MW00826370

THE ART OF SWORD COMBAT

THE ART OF SWORD COMBAT

A 1568 GERMAN TREATISE ON SWORDMANSHIP

JOACHIM MEYER

Translated by Jeffrey L. Forgeng

Frontline Books, London

The Art of Sword Combat
A 1568 German Treatise on Swordmanship

First published in Great Britain in 2016
and reprinted in 2017, 2018 and 2020 by
Frontline Books
An imprint of Pen & Sword Books Limited
47 Church Street
Barnsley
South Yorkshire
S70 2AS

ISBN 978 1 47387 675 0

Library of Congress Cataloging-in Publication Data available

Typeset by JCS Publishing Services Ltd, www.jcs-publishing.co.uk
Printed and bound in the UK by TJ International Ltd, Padstow, Cornwall

Pen & Sword Books Limited incorporates the imprints of Atlas, Archaeology, Aviation, Discovery, Family
History, Fiction, History, Maritime, Military, Military Classics, Politics, Select, Transport, True Crime,
Air World, Frontline Publishing, Leo Cooper, Remember When, Seaforth Publishing, The Praetorian
Press, Wharncliffe Local History, Wharncliffe Transport,Wharncliffe True Crime and White Owl.
For a complete list of Pen & Sword titles please contact
PEN & SWORD BOOKS LIMITED
47 Church Street, Barnsley, South Yorkshire S70 2AS, United Kingdom
E-mail: enquiries@pen-and-sword.co.uk
Website: www.pen-and-sword.co.uk
Or
PEN AND SWORD BOOKS
1950 Lawrence Rd, Havertown, PA 19083, USA
E-mail: Uspen-and-sword@casematepublishers.com
Website: www.penandswordbooks.com

Contents

Acknowledgements

When I started working on Joachim Meyer in 2000, I was very much alone in the enterprise; it has been gratifying to witness the emergence of a community of people contributing to our shared knowledge of the sixteenth-century master. I would like to thank Lunds Universitetsbibliothek, not only for gracious permission to reproduce the images from the manuscript, but also for the consistently exemplary assistance they provided throughout our interactions on this project. Thanks are also due to the Archives de la ville et de l'Eurométropole de Strasbourg for permission to reproduce the image at the head of Olivier Dupuis's article. I would particularly like to acknowledge the contributions of Dupuis himself, whose work in the Strasbourg archives has done so much to put a human face on the author, and who has graciously allowed my translation of his article on Meyer to be published as part of this work. I would also like to thank Roger Norling, the force behind the Facebook page calling for the reprint of my 2006 translation of Meyer's *Art of Combat*, and a valuable Meyer scholar in his own right; and Heike Tröger and Daniel Faustmann, who have generously shared the fruits of their work on Meyer's Rostock manuscript. Finally I would like to give special thanks to William R. Short, a driving force in the Higgins Armory Sword Guild during the museum's glorious final decade and a half; Bill's tireless efforts in our shared undertakings did more than I can say to contribute to the quality and productivity of my work during my time at the Higgins Armory.

Introduction

Any account of the combat treatises (*Fechtbücher* in German) that document the traditional martial arts practices of the Middle Ages and Renaissance must rank Joachim Meyer in the top tier of importance. Meyer's published treatise, the *Kunst des Fechtens* ('Art of Combat'), first printed in 1570, stands as a uniquely detailed and systematic encyclopedia of the combat traditions that Meyer's generation inherited from the Middle Ages.[1] His work remained influential for more than a century after his death, with numerous authors borrowing from Meyer or mentioning his work, both within the German-speaking world and beyond it. Today, international enthusiasm for Meyer's work among modern practitioners of historical combat testifies to Meyer's intelligence, clarity, and efficacy in tackling the challenge of reducing the complexities of combat into words and images.[2]

Meyer's significance has been further enhanced by some striking new discoveries. In the past decade, the author has been transformed from a shadowy figure known only from his one published work to a well-documented historical personality whose life, career, and writings can be traced through the written record, including two recently discovered manuscripts of martial arts material created in whole or in part by Meyer.[3]

The manuscript translated here, Lunds Universitetsbibliothek Msc. A 4o 2, offers important data about both Meyer's personal story and the martial arts as he practised, taught, and documented them. In part, the manuscript represents an early version of his published *Art of Combat*: the first section, covering techniques for the longsword, overlaps heavily with the material he would eventually publish. However, the relationship is much more distant for the sections on the dusack and the rapier: not only do they offer substantially different content than in the 1570 *Fechtbuch*, but in some important areas the manuscript helps elucidate the contents of the published work. For clarity, and in recognition of the substantially different content of more than half of the manuscript, the text is here titled *The Art of Sword Combat*.

Meyer's Life

Since the publication of my translation of Meyer's *Art of Combat* in 2006, much has been learned about Meyer's biography, thanks in large measure to Olivier Dupuis (see Appendix B) - though, as Dupuis notes in his article, further research may turn up additional information in the foreseeable future. Meyer spent most of his adult years in Strassburg, where he published his *Art of Combat*, but Strassburg records indicate that he was born in Basel.[4] A Joachim Meyer is recorded as being born in Basel in 1537, the son of Jacob Meyer, a stationer, and Anna Freund. The place, date, and social status are consistent with everything that is known about Meyer's life, but the name is not unique, and the identification remains hypothetical. Nonetheless, given that Meyer married in 1560, and that the typical age for first marriage in men of his class was in the early to mid-20s, he is likely to have been born in the latter half of the 1530s.[5]

We can be reasonably sure that Meyer grew up in advantaged middle-class circumstances of the day: his family had the means to secure him an apprenticeship, as well as a solid education, as evidenced by his literary skill and familiarity with historical sources, particularly evident in the preface to the published *Art of Combat*. Given Meyer's residence exclusively in Protestant environments and his consistent association with Protestant patrons, we can assume that he was himself a Protestant.

The earliest certain documentation of Meyer's life is the record of his marriage to Apollonia Rülmann in the parish of St William in Strassburg on 4 June 1560. Strassburg in the 1560s was a small city of about 22,000 inhabitants. Since the Middle Ages it had been a Free City of the Holy Roman Empire, nominally falling within the Empire's jurisdiction but essentially self-governed by a city council known as 'the Council and the Twenty-One'. Like Basel, Strassburg was located on the Rhine (actually just off the river, with a system of waterways connecting the city to the Rhine itself). The two cities were closely bound to each other economically and culturally – in addition to the ties of Rhenish trade, both were important Protestant centres in the German-speaking world. Meyer's migration from Basel to Strassburg was far from an unusual life story.[6]

Meyer's wife, Apollonia, was the widow of Jacob Wittgaw; her late husband had been a baker and citizen of the town. Through right of the widow, Meyer was himself admitted to citizenship six days after his

Jost Amman's Ständebuch of 1568 depicts the shop of a cutler (Messerschmidt) in Meyer's day. (sig. R3r)

marriage. The marriage record specifies that Meyer was a cutler, and the record of his citizenship assigns him to the Company of Smiths, which served as the general guild for a variety of metalworking crafts.[7]

Meyer's marriage to a well-established widow was a stereotypical story for young men of his class. With relatively high mortality rates, widowhood was not a rare event even for fairly young women, and in the male-dominated world of the 1500s it was advantageous for a widow to find a new husband to help keep her household financially stable. Widows actually accounted for about 40 per cent of brides in Strassburg during the 1560s, although the figure was somewhat elevated by an epidemic of the plague in 1564.[8] For a young man of Meyer's position, marriage to a citizen's widow brought with it the rights of citizenship, allowing him to set up shop for himself, leaving behind the hand-to-mouth existence of a hired journeyman for a position of relative stability and comfort, perhaps even with prospects for social and economic advancement.[9]

In addition to his day job as a cutler, Meyer was an experienced practitioner of the martial arts. Multiple entries in the minutes of the city council over the course of the 1560s document requests from Meyer for permission to hold public fencing competitions (*Fechtschulen*). The earliest of these, in 1561, mentions another fencer, Christoph Elias, who is described as having studied under Meyer, implying that Meyer was already an advanced practitioner at this time.

Over the course of the 1560s Meyer was clearly becoming a significant player in the fencing scene. In addition to his activities as a teacher and organiser of prizefights, he was seeking out both German and foreign sources of knowledge on the martial arts, as alluded to in the published *Art of Combat* (2.50r–v) and on fol. 123r of Meyer's 'Rostock Fechtbuch' (see Appendix A). He eventually began producing written treatises of his own, including the present manuscript, parts of the Rostock Fechtbuch, and the published *Art of Combat*.

By the latter half of the decade Meyer was beginning to make himself known to important aficionados of the art outside of Strassburg. The Lund manuscript is dedicated to Graf Otto von Solms-Sonnewalde, and indicates that the count was a pupil of Meyer's. In later years Otto would enter military service with Pfalzgraf Johann Casimir of the Palatinate-Simmern (1543–1592), to whom Meyer dedicated the printed *Art of Combat* in 1570.[10] By this time Meyer also appears to have made contact with Graf Stephan Heinrich von Everstein (1533–1613), who is mentioned in connection with the rapier content in Meyer's Rostock Fechtbuch (fol. 123r).

The Lund manuscript is likely to have played a part in Meyer's strategy for self-promotion as a master of the martial arts, a strategy he further pursued with his lavish published volume of 1570. The printed *Art of Combat* was richly illustrated with woodblock prints: art historians attribute the designs stylistically to Tobias Stimmer, a Swiss artist who was active in both Switzerland and Strassburg during this period. The woodcuts were executed by several cutters, including Stimmer's brother Hans Christoph.[11] The woodcuts made the book expensive to produce, and Meyer had to take a loan of 300 crowns in order to finance it – the figure represented several times the annual income of a craftsman like Meyer.[12] But his efforts to win a reputation were bearing fruit. He travelled to Speyer in 1570, probably in conjunction with the Imperial Diet (*Reichstag*) that took place there that summer, which would have afforded an excellent opportunity to show his recent publication to prospective patrons among the German aristocracy. The search proved successful: at Speyer he contracted with Duke Johann-Albrecht I of Mecklenburg-Schwerin (1525–1576) to serve as fencing master at the Duke's court. In addition to income from the position, Meyer believed that the court would provide an excellent market for his newly published work, which he thought he might sell for over 30 florins a copy. He shipped his books to Schwerin, and set out in person in January 1571.

The journey, 800 km (500 miles) across northern Germany in the middle of winter, seems to have broken Meyer's health. He arrived at Schwerin on 10 February, and died on 24 February, exactly one year after the date of his preface to *The Art of Combat*. Meyer's brother-in-law, Antoni Rülmann, took responsibility for Apollonia's affairs, and sought the aid of the Strassburg city council in getting Duke Johann-Albrecht to return Meyer's property, particularly the books, which were some of his most valuable assets. The Duke returned Meyer's personal effects and sent some money to his widow, but reported that the chest of books had been inspected, and the contents were ruined by water damage. One may wonder whether the Duke was being entirely truthful. Certainly there is cause to suspect that he quietly appropriated Meyer's Rostock Fechtbuch: it ended up in the ducal library, through which it would eventually come to Rostock University. The woodblocks for *The Art of Combat* were apparently sold to settle Meyer's estate; by 1600 they were in Augsburg, where they were used to print the second edition of the work.[13]

Meyer's Works

Until recently Meyer's only known work was the printed *Art of Combat*. First published in Strassburg in 1570, the book was well received by contemporaries. It was reprinted in a virtually identical edition in Augsburg in 1600, and heavily cribbed by Jacob Sutor for his *New Kunstliches Fechtbuch* (1612) and by Theodor Verolinus for *Der Kunstliche Fechter* (1679). Meyer is singled out for mention in Heinrich von Günterode's

Latin treatise on martial arts of 1579, and quoted in Christoff Rösener's florilegium of martial arts verses of 1589.[14] The work even received international recognition. Meyer is the only German among the masters listed in the seventeenth-century fencing treatises by Narváez, Pallavicini, and Marcelli - indeed almost the only master in these lists who is not Iberian or Italian.[15] Oddly, Pallavicini's citations of Meyer bear no resemblance to the published work, and may derive from some other author; but the recent discovery of Meyer's *Sword Combat* and his Rostock Fechtbuch reminds us that there is still much to be learned about the *Fechtbuch* corpus, and Meyer's works could have been more extensive than those known to us today.[16]

Meyer's Rostock Fechtbuch

Most *Fechtbücher* are compendia of miscellaneous texts and illustrations copied or adapted from prior sources, and Meyer's Rostock Fechtbuch is among the last major manuscripts in this tradition. Rostock University Library Mss. var. 82 is a paper manuscript measuring 20.5 cm (8 in) by 17 cm (7 in). There are at least four distinct hands, all from the sixteenth century, including one that is probably Meyer's own (fols. 5r, 123r–127r, and the marginal notes on fols. 112r–121r); this hand twice names Meyer as the author of the manuscript's section on the rapier (fols. 5r and 123r). Fol. 123r dates the rapier section to 1570, though the manuscript as a whole was probably compiled over a period of time leading up to that date, and much or most of it may predate Meyer's ownership of the codex - the sections that mention Meyer are on a different paper from the rest, and Meyer may have added them to a pre-existing manuscript. The manuscript was formerly part of the library of the dukes of Mecklenburg-Schwerin, almost certainly having come into their hands through Meyer's relocation to Schwerin in 1571: it was in Johann Albrecht's library by 1573; in the 1700s it came to the Bützow University Library, relocating to Rostock with the merger of the Bützow and Rostock university libraries in 1789.[17]

The manuscript includes material from multiple sources, much of it composed in the fifteenth and even fourteenth centuries, and documenting combat arts that were largely obsolete by Meyer's day. The major groups of material in the manuscript can be broken down as follows:

- *Liechtenauer Commentaries*: At some point, probably around the mid-1300s, a combat-master named Johannes Liechtenauer composed versified summaries of his techniques for unarmoured longsword, armoured combat, and mounted combat. These verses were later furnished with explanatory 'glosses' in prose, the most important of which appear to have taken shape in the early 1400s. The glossed verses survive in three primary variants: in the 'Starhemberg', 'Lew', and 'Ringeck' manuscripts of the mid-1400s. The Rostock Fechtbuch includes two separate versions of the commentaries on Liechtenauer's longsword verses, one in the 'Ringeck' family, the other in the 'Lew' family; the former appears to derive from a lost illustrated exemplar. There are also copies of the 'Lew' and 'Ringeck' versions of the commentaries on Liechtenauer's verses on armoured combat and the 'Lew' version of the commentaries on Liechtenauer's mounted-combat verses.[18]

- *Leckiüchner's Swordplay Treatise*: Johannes Leckiüchner's 1478 treatise describes techniques for the *lange Messer* – a single-handed, single-edged utility sword. The weapon had fallen out of use by Meyer's day, but its techniques were applicable to any single-handed sword. The Rostock text is adapted from Leckiüchner, and presented as combat with the 'rapier'. It is accompanied by marginal annotations that may be in Meyer's own hand.[19]
- *Miscellaneous Combat Texts*: The manuscript includes a grouping of shorter materials, mostly from the fifteenth century, and mostly having parallels in the Starhemberg manuscript and related *Fechtbücher*. Among these are the 'Liegnitzer' text on the 'shortened sword' – here attributed to Martin Hundfelt as in the Speyer Fechtbuch of 1491; Martin Siber's 'Six Passes', again paralleled in the Speyer manuscript; Martin Huntfelt's verses on mounted combat; and Andre Liegnitzer's sword-and-buckler plays.[20]
- *Dagger*: A substantial section of dagger plays of unknown origin, having close relationships with content in Paulus Hector Mair's compendium of c. 1555.[21]
- *Meyer's Rapier-Combat*: A brief and incomplete text on the rapier, ascribed to Meyer, and probably in his hand (see Appendix A).[22] Related to this in subject matter at least are the rapier diagrams and explanatory texts, in a different hand, on fols. 1v–3v.

Meyer's Art of Sword Combat

The Lund manuscript evidently represents an earlier stage in the development of what would become Meyer's published *Art of Combat*. The published version repeats almost word-for-word most of the section on the longsword, about a third of the manuscript. The sections on the dusack and rapier were substantially rewritten for the printed version, though their overall structure is still recognisable; the published book also adds sections on dagger, wrestling, and staff weapons. Illustrations as well as text are echoed in the printed work. Most of the Lund images reappear in some form in the 1570 *Art of Combat*, though the printed woodcuts group the individual pairs of fighters into bustling training scenes in fanciful Italianate environments.

Longsword Image O from The Art of Combat – *cf. fols. 16v, 37r of the manuscript.*
Worcester Art Museum (MA), The John Woodman Higgins Collection, 2014.583.

The manuscript is undated, but must predate the published book. Modern references to the manuscript sometimes date it to 1560, but this is assuredly too early.[23] Created as a presentation copy for a noble patron by skilled artists and scribes, it must have been expensive to commission. Meyer did not become a citizen of Strassburg until 1560, and until he achieved citizenship Meyer could hardly have accumulated the means to produce such a text - or the connections to find someone else to pay for it.

Further evidence for a later date can be found in the biography of the manuscript's recipient, Count Otto von Solms, lord of Münzenberg and Sonnewalde (1550–1612). Otto was only ten years old in 1560, rather young to be training at the level implied by this text, and not yet at the stage of studying the liberal arts, as referenced in Meyer's preface (fol. 4v). Later in the decade, around 1568, Otto spent some time at the Protestant Academy at Strassburg, which would match perfectly the situation implied by the preface.[24] The preface further suggests that, at the time the manuscript was created, Otto's study with Meyer was over, or soon would be, probably dating its production around the end of his time in Strassburg. The manuscript may have been presented to Otto before he left, or perhaps delivered to him on a subsequent stage of his travels, which took him to the Savoy region, and then to France, England, and Italy.[25]

After the Count's death the manuscript remained in his family until 1642, when Swedish forces under the command of Hans Christoff von Königsmarck captured Sonnewalde. Johannes Levi von Sommerlad, left in charge of the Swedish garrison at Sonnewalde, plundered the valuables of the castle and town, sending home spoils of war that included the counts' library. The exact fate of the books during the following year is unknown, but by 1643 they were evidently in the hands of the Sparre family, ending up in the possession of Count Axel Sparre (1652–1728). At Axel's death, his widow Anna Maria Falkenberg gifted the library to her nephew Melker Falkenberg, who donated it to the Lund University Library in 1780.[26]

The manuscript consists of eighty-eight paper leaves in horizontal quarto format, measuring about 29 cm (11½ in) by 20.5 cm (8 in); at least one original leaf appears to be missing, between fols. 5 and 6. The binding is covered in worn and faded velvet, with leather down the spine, and fabric ties to secure the codex closed; the edges of the paperblock show the remains of gilding. The binding is old, but more recent than the original manuscript, perhaps dating to the period of the manuscript's donation to Lund University. Probably at the time of this rebinding, the pages were trimmed on the upper and outer edges, and the edges gilded or regilded: on many pages, the original ink folio numbers at the upper right have been cut off; the margins are asymmetric, and some illustrations are asymmetrically placed; and in a few cases (e.g. fol. 14r) the illustration has been slightly cut off. On the inside cover is the original Lund shelfmark of the manuscript, B. N. MSC. N. 37, as well as the current one, Msc. A. 4o 2, along with the bookplate of Lund University Library.

There are thirty watercolour illustrations, and seven diagrams in ink. The fencing hall scene at the beginning of the manuscript is executed in mezzotint style; all other colour illustrations are polychromatic, with outlining and accents in ink, and white highlighting on some of the fighting pairs. Traces of pencil sketching can be seen on some illustrations, in particular fol. 14r, where the sketch is offset to the right of the final illustration. Most of the illustrations are referenced somewhere in the text, and most reappear in the woodcuts of the printed version, although variations in the rendering of the figures make some easier to recognise than others. One or two illustrations are lacking (fols. 7v and perhaps 29r), which is surprising for an otherwise well-executed presentation manuscript.

The foliation of the manuscript is slightly complex at the beginning, due to the loss and reordering of some leaves. A modern series of pencilled folio numbers replaces older numbers in ink that have been partially or fully lost on many pages due to trimming. Fol. 1r bears only the Swedish inscription 'Joachim Meyers Fäktbok', with nothing on fol. 1v; this leaf is probably not original to the manuscript, though it may replace a lost title page. The following two leaves, bearing Count Otto's coat of arms on the verso and a fencing scene on the recto respectively, have been reversed from their original order: they are numbered 2 and 3 in pencil, but the original ink numbers read 2 and 1 (the latter is a bit hard to decipher). This translation restores the original order, which corresponds to the ordering of the frontmatter in the printed edition, where the title page includes a fencing hall scene on the recto, with the patron's coat of arms on the verso, facing the dedicatory letter.

The inked numbers lack a folio 5, which would have fallen between the dedicatory letter and the longsword section; it may have included some introductory matter on the longsword or on the art of combat in general, as in the printed version. The following two leaves, bearing the pencilled numbers 6 and 7, have again been reversed, since their ink numbers are 7 and 6 (again, the latter is a bit hard to make out). The translation restores the original order, which corresponds slightly better to the published version, as well as providing a better flow into the beginning of fol. 8r. At some point between folios 14 and 22 the inked numbers appear to skip one, but there is no obvious break in the text, and this may be a simple numbering error - it is difficult to be certain because many of the ink numbers are cut off in this section.[27] Similarly, the pencilled numbers skip 79, so that the ink and pencil numbers from 80 to the end once again match each other, and are both one greater than the actual folio number.

There are two distinguishable hands: the A-hand is responsible for the preface and introductory matter on the longsword (fols. 4r–9r), two techniques at the end of the longsword (fols. 38v–39v), the section on the dusack (fols. 43r–64v), and the final section of the rapier (fols. 82r–88v); this hand can be recognised by its more elegant and florid style - for example, the gracefully looped d's. The B-hand is responsible for the longsword verses and commentary (fols. 10r–38v) and most of the section on the rapier (fols. 68r–82r). It is more workaday, with fewer rounded flourishes on the letters (compare the generally simpler d's). Neither hand matches Meyer's own hand as found in his Rostock Fechtbook, which is hardly surprising: one would expect a presentation manuscript of this sort to be produced by professional scriveners. It is worth noting the implication that both this manuscript and the published *Art of Combat* must derive from now-lost drafts in Meyer's own hand; there were presumably also sketches that formed the basis of both the manuscript and published illustrations.

The Weapons

The Longsword

Like most *Fechtbuch* authors, Meyer begins with the longsword (G *langes Schwert* or *Langschwert*; Meyer usually just calls it the *Schwert*), a weapon derived from the classical sidearm of the late medieval knight. Sometimes termed a 'hand-and-a-half sword' or 'bastard sword', the longsword was designed to be usable with either one or two hands, an important feature for someone who fought both on horseback and on foot. For armoured combat on foot, the longsword was normally held in the 'halfsword' position, with the secondary hand on the blade, turning the weapon into a short spear that could more effectively target the gaps in the opponent's armour. Halfsword techniques were also applied in unarmoured combat, but here they typically served to facilitate various forms of grappling (cf. fols. 30v, 33r, 35r, 37r, 38v.1).[28]

By Meyer's day, armoured combat on foot was no longer common, and the longsword had lost its military importance, but a specialised sporting version designed for safety continued in use, particularly in German-speaking areas, from at least the 1400s into the 1700s.[29] This is the weapon shown in Meyer's illustrations, recognisable by its rounded tip and broad section at the ricasso (termed a *Schilt*, 'shield'). The original example shown opposite, dating to Meyer's period, is towards the larger end of surviving examples.[30] The blade length is 107.3 cm (42¼ in), with a hilt of 34 cm (13⅜ in); the crossbars are 30 cm (11¾ in) across, and weight is just under 2.25 kg (5 lb). The blade is about 2 cm ($\frac{13}{16}$ in) wide at the base, with a robust thickness of 7 mm (¼ in) at the base thinning to a mere 0.8 mm ($^1/_{32}$ in) at the tip. As with the examples in the manuscript, it has an ovoid pommel and simple crossbar with rounded ends – the rounded surface at all four extremities of the weapon is doubtless a safety feature. The cusps on the *Schilt* of the example shown here relate to two-handed swords that had a pair of projections at this point (sometimes called *Parierhaken*), serving to protect the hand when it was slipped onto the blade in techniques like those illustrated on fol. 39r.[31]

The strong taper and thin foible of these fencing swords allowed the blade to flex, a feature visible on fol. 18v; some of Meyer's techniques may deliberately exploit the flexibility of the blade by whipping it around the opponent's sword to deliver a hit (see Glossary s.v. **slinging**). Exploiting this flex would require hitting with the flat of the blade, an entirely viable option within the rules of longsword fencing: victory was accorded to the first combatant to draw blood, something quite feasible with a flicking strike from the thin, spatulate tip of the weapon.

The bulk of Meyer's longsword section consists of his verses on the weapon along with his commentary on

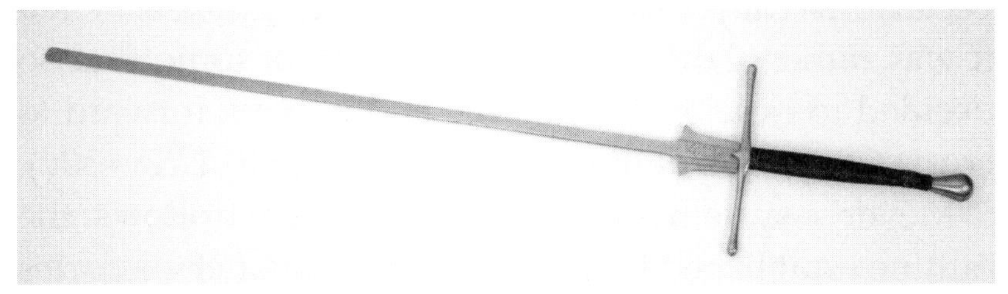

A fencing longsword of Meyer's period.
Worcester Art Museum (MA), The John Woodman Higgins Collection, 2015.13.
Image © Worcester Art Museum, All Rights Reserved.

their meaning, a standard format for longsword treatises dating back to the 1300s. Verses of this sort were known in German as a *Zettel* (here translated as 'epitome'); the commentaries were called 'glosses'. Meyer's *Zettel* and glosses derive ultimately from the tradition of Johannes Liechtenauer, the fourteenth-century master whose glossed verses provided the basis and model for much of the *Fechtbuch* corpus. Meyer was familiar with these medieval sources - he cites the Liechtenauer verses and glosses on fol. 8r, and copies of some of the relevant texts appear in his Rostock Fechtbuch.[32]

Meyer's glossed *Zettel* (fols. 10r–39v) largely matches Part 3 of the longsword treatise in the printed *Art of Combat* (fols. 1.45v–61r), though there are some revisions, reorderings, and additions in the published text. Meyer's introductory section on the weapon (fols. 6r–9r) was substantially expanded as Parts 1 and 2 of the printed version (fols. 1.1r–44v) - for example, the lists of guards, cuts, and other techniques were expanded to offer definitions of each. However, some material has been lost in this section of the manuscript, so it is impossible to tell just how extensive the revision was. The greatest divergence between the manuscript and published versions lies between fols. 32v and 35v - probably because, as Meyer says at the end of the passage, he felt it was rather short for such an important topic, and so decided to expand the material and move it forward to create Chapter 10 of the published book (fols. 1.27v–30v).

Meyer's system of longsword combat follows the outline established by Johannes Liechtenauer centuries before. The list of techniques on fol. 7r would largely have been familiar to Meyer's fourteenth- and fifteenth-century predecessors, including the organising concepts of four Chief Guards and five Master Cuts, both of which feature in Liechtenauer's verses. Nonetheless, there have been some innovations – the notion of eight secondary guards, for example, appears to be Meyer's own (though the guards themselves are found in medieval sources); the six Secret Cuts are also new: previous sources use the term synonymously for the Master Cuts, and the cuts Meyer names in this group are rare or absent in earlier sources.

Meyer would elaborate on this system, without significantly altering it, in the printed *Art of Combat*. Perhaps the only slight difference worth noting lies in the ambiguous status of the thrust. The printed *Art of Combat* specifies that thrusting is no longer permitted in longsword combat (fols. 1.3v, 8r, 10v, 2.50r), a detail not mentioned in the manuscript. Indeed, fol. 31r of *The Art of Sword Combat* references the thrust as an option, whereas the equivalent passage in the printed version omits the thrust. However, this is likely just a holdover from the traditional language of the Liechtenauer school, where the thrust, cut, and slice are the three proverbial modes of attack.[33] Indeed, the only technique that actually uses a thrust is 21r.4, which remains unchanged in the printed version. In both cases, the thrust may be seen as a means of provoking a response rather than being delivered with the intention to hit.

Dusack

The dusack (G *Duseken*), like the longsword, was purely a sporting weapon, though, as Meyer's title for the section indicates, the techniques could theoretically be applied to any single-handed sword. The dusack emerged in the 1500s as a sporting derivative of the *langes Messer*, a single-handed, single-edged sword of the late Middle Ages; like the fencing longsword, it continued in use into the 1700s.[34] Elsewhere, Meyer identifies the dusack as a characteristically German weapon (*Art of Combat*, 2.1r): the weapon is indeed well documented in German sources, and rare elsewhere. However, the name suggests the possibility of Czech influence, being derived from the Czech *tesák*; and the appearance of two of Meyer's dusack combatants in distinctive eastern European attire may reflect an awareness that the weapon had connections east of the German-speaking zone (see fols. 53r and 57r).

Unlike the longsword, surviving dusacks akin to those illustrated by Meyer have yet to be discovered. This is doubtless due to the material: the dusack was normally made of leather or wood, as suggested by the light brown colour of the weapons in the manuscript, contrasting with the metallic grey of the swords.[35] Meyer's dusacks appear to be about 65–75 cm (25–30 in) long. They may have had a small curved hand-guard on the outside of the hilt, deriving from the *Wehrnagel*, a similar projection on the hilt of the *Messer*. This feature is hinted at by the left-hand figure on fol. 54r and attested by other visual sources.[36]

Meyer's system of dusack combat derives from that of the *langes Messer*. The techniques of the *Messer* had been given their authoritative form in Johannes Leckküchner's treatise of 1478 - another medieval text familiar to Meyer, since a version is included in his Rostock Fechtbuch.[37] The techniques inherited from Leckküchner paralleled those of the longsword, though the guards and Master Cuts had different names in the one-handed version, and by Meyer's day the execution of the cuts seems to have diverged from their longsword equivalents; indeed the very concept of Master Cuts is absent from Meyer's dusack texts, although it is still present for the longsword. Curiously, Meyer's list of dusack cuts in the manuscript diverges both from the traditional scheme and from his published *Art of Combat*, as laid out below.

Longsword Master Cuts	**Leckküchner *Messer* Master Cuts**	**Meyer Dusack**
Wrath Cut (*Zornhaw*)	Wrath Cut (*Zornhaw*)	Wrath Cut (*Zornhaw*)
Squinter Cut (*Schielerhaw*)	Constrainer (*Zwinger*)	Constrainer Cut (*Zwingerhaw*)
Scalper Cut (*Scheitelerhaw*)	Danger Cut (*Geferhaw*)	Present in 1570, not mentioned in Lund
Thwart Cut (*Zwerchhaw*)	Anger Cut (*Entrüsthaw*)	Present in 1570, not mentioned in Lund
Crooked Cut (*Krumphaw*)	Waker (*Wecker*)	1570 and Lund both include a 'Crooked Cut' and a 'Waker', though the former has nothing to do with its longsword equivalent, and the latter is at best weakly related to the longsword Crooked Cut

The discrepancies may in part reflect rapidly changing practices in the use of the dusack during Meyer's day, a conclusion that could be supported by comparison to other sixteenth-century texts on the weapon. As early as 1516, Andre Paurenfeindt's treatise diverges dramatically from the Leckùchner tradition. His section on the *Messer*, depicting transitional weapons somewhere between Leckùchner's weapon and the later sixteenth-century dusack, mentions none of Leckùchner's Master Cuts.[38] Paulus Hector Mair's dusack techniques, dating to about 1550–5, reference the Wrath Cut a few times, the Danger, Constrainer, and Anger cuts once each, and do not mention the Waker at all.[39] Such fluctuations among the texts could be influenced by the tension between the received authority of Leckùchner and the physicality of a substantially different weapon. The Master Cuts in part worked because of the length of the longsword and *Messer* – the Thwart Cut, for example, protected the head with the forte while striking with the foible. The shorter dusack was less suited for such techniques, perhaps accounting for the rarity of the Anger Cut in the dusack texts.

The discrepancies between Meyer's own texts on the dusack may also reflect the evolution of his thinking about this weapon form. Meyer's section on the dusack is the least clearly structured part of the manuscript. He begins with general concepts and principles – guards, openings, cuts – but the ordering of the following techniques seems largely associative. This may be why this material was so heavily reworked in the printed edition – certainly the organisational structure of the 1570 version is considerably clearer. Nonetheless, there is valuable content in the manuscript that never made it into the printed redaction – the discussion of the nature of the guards (fols. 43r–44v) helps elucidate their role in Meyer's system of combat, and the section on 'driving' (fols. 63v–64v) adds significantly to Meyer's remarkable repertoire of training drills, a feature found in very few early combat treatises (cf. Meyer, *Art of Combat*, 2.4 ff.).

Rapier

Of the weapons covered in the manuscript, only the rapier (G *Rappier*) was used for earnest combat in Meyer's day. The weapon had originated in Mediterranean Europe, and was a relatively recent arrival in German-speaking lands. Meyer is only the second German author to describe its use, the first being Paulus Hector Mair around the early 1550s. Even as late as the printed edition of 1570, Meyer feels he needs to justify the inclusion of this foreign weapon amidst the traditional repertoire of German arms.[40]

The rapier was a civilian weapon, worn with ordinary clothing as part of daily wear, and serving for self-defence and duelling, as well as for a fashionable sport favoured by socially ambitious young men of the day. The real-life applications of this weapon are reflected in the manuscript, which discusses techniques for defending oneself with this weapon against an attacker with a staff weapon, and how to use a cloak in the off-hand.[41]

Rapiers of Meyer's period typically have a blade length in the neighbourhood of 100 cm (40 in), weighing around 1.25 kg (2.75 lb); this is about the length suggested by Meyer's illustrations. The rapier blade tended to be a bit longer and thinner than that of a military sword, improving the weapon's reach and thrusting capacity at the cost of robustness and cutting power, but the differences between the weapons in Meyer's period were not as pronounced as they would later become; nor is the distinction between rapiers and military-style swords an absolute typological boundary. The weapons shown in the manuscript have round pommels, straight crossbars with rounded ends, side rings, and knuckleguards, and a stepped profile comparable to that of the longswords, suggesting that these too are flexible fencing weapons (cf. fol. 2.106r in the printed version).[42]

As with the dusack, Meyer's system for the rapier appears to be in flux, borrowing ideas from multiple directions - from the longsword, from the dusack, and from other swordsmen - and experimenting with new syntheses. The rapid evolution of Meyer's thinking about the rapier can again be seen by comparing his various texts on the subject, which are profoundly different from each other. The Rostock Fechtbuch includes a treatise on the 'rapier' that is actually just an adaptation of Lecküchner's verses - the annotations in the margin are probably in Meyer's hand, suggesting that he was a reader rather than the author of the text itself. The fragmentary 1570 treatise on rapier combat ascribed to Meyer in his Rostock manuscript bears little resemblance to either of Meyer's other rapier texts (see Appendix A).

Meyer's printed *Art of Combat* text on the rapier overlaps the present one in structure and content: the printed book, like the manuscript, uses the guards as an organising principle for structuring the text, an idea that appears to have influenced Meyer's revision of the long-sword section in his published version; the appended material on self-defence scenarios is echoed in the 1570 version; and a few techniques from the manuscript reappear in the published book (cf. 72v.3, 77v.2, 87v.1).

But like the dusack section, there is minimal word-for-word repetition of content. It is also interesting to note differences in the system itself – for example, the Low Guard, prominent in the printed text, is missing from the manuscript. There are also curious features of the vocabulary in this section: the terms *Gefess* ('hilt', which Meyer elsewhere usually calls the *Gehiltz*), *gegen thall* ('downward', in place of *undersich*), *Wehr* ('weapon', in place of naming the type of weapon), and the use of *durch* in expressions like 'through the Irongate/Plow/Middle Cut' are rather different from the vocabulary of the longsword and dusack sections of the manuscript, and of the published *Art of Combat*. These discrepancies might suggest that the present text is substantially influenced by someone other than Meyer himself.

Overall, the printed version is more orderly in its presentation and more extensive. Nonetheless, there is once again significant material here that is lacking in the published book; for example, the lists of defences available from each guard, and the 'brawling' sequences that again offer a rare example of sixteenth-century training practices. Overall, while the manuscript is – predictably – less polished than the published *Art of Combat*, its creativity and intelligence confirm Meyer's stature as a thinker of primary importance in the history of martial arts culture.

The Translation

The parameters of this translation remain largely consistent with those I laid out for Meyer's printed *Art of Combat* a decade ago. My goal then was to offer a clean, honest translation, rendering the content into reasonably idiomatic modern English – to the degree that the text's age and technical subject matter permitted – without imposing my own interpretations, particularly in passages where the original was open to multiple readings. Revisiting my work a decade later, I still find the translation readable and illuminating, and I discover meanings and implications that have become clearer to me from a decade of further study in the field, a good sign that I was on the right track.

All terms are rendered into English; in some places the original German terms are given in square brackets. Interpreting Meyer's technical vocabulary into English naturally requires the construction of a systematic translation scheme, documented in the Glossary at the end of this book. It must be borne in mind that the connotations of any given word in English do not necessarily match those of the German original, and the sense of the words must be understood relative to their use in the text, rather than from the possible implications of the English rendition.

Folio numbers are given in angled brackets; as is common with manuscripts, numbers are assigned to each leaf, not each side, so the leaf number is followed by 'r' (*recto*, i.e. front) or 'v' (*verso*, i.e. back). Since the word order of German is different from English, the location of the page breaks is not always exact. The folio numbers roughly correspond to the modern pencilled numbers, except where the order of the folios has been restored to that of Meyer's original book. That book, and this translation, begins on fol. 2r.

Meyer's longsword verses (the *Zettel*) are set apart typographically, and I have inserted line numbers in square brackets based on the printed version of 1570. Meyer appears to have some implicit system of numbering the verses, as referenced on fol. 11v, but this system seems to count each block of verse as two verses - whether it numbers two lines or four - and I have not tried to reproduce it.

Since the analysis of the *Fechtbücher* will in the long term involve a great deal of study and comparison of individual combat sequences (*Stücke*, here translated as 'techniques'), these have been set apart typographically in the text, and I have inserted reference numbers in the margin to make them easier to identify. The numeration system is based on the page on which the sequence begins, followed by a sequential number based on the order of sequences on that page, e.g. 16r.2 designates the second sequence that begins on folio 16 recto. It is not always a straightforward matter to decide what actually constitutes a sequence, or where one sequence ends and another begins, but over the years I have found this system of reference extremely useful in assisting textual analysis. The marginal numeration for the sequences also cross-references them with their counterparts in the 1570 edition, where clear parallels exist.

The translation ignores simple scribal errors, such as dittography, and does not systematically record alterations of the text by the scribe or author (e.g. cancellations, insertions, etc.). Footnotes are supplied in the few places where the author's intent is not entirely clear. Square brackets indicate places where the translation deviates substantially from the manuscript. In a few places editorial headings have been inserted in square brackets to assist the reader in navigating the text, paralleling headings elsewhere supplied by Meyer himself.

Some noteworthy differences between the text here and in the published *Art of Combat* are flagged in footnotes, but the two texts are not systematically compared. Also, where necessary, I have added explanatory captions to the illustrations – these are set apart by italics.

Notes

1 For editions and translations of Meyer, see the Bibliography. For surveys of the *Fechtbuch* tradition in general, see my introduction to Meyer, *Art of Combat*, pp. 11–16; Forgeng, 'Owning the Art'; Forgeng and Kiermayer, 'The Chivalric Art'; Hils, *Liechtenauers Kunst*; Leng, *Katalog*.

2 In addition to modern editions and translations of Meyer listed in the Bibliography, any web search, especially for audiovisual content, will quickly reveal a plethora of material inspired by enthusiasm for Meyer's work.

3 Hils's *Liechtenauers Kunst* documents the corpus of these texts as known in 1985, prior to the reinvigoration of the field in the 1990s. Quite a number of new manuscripts have surfaced since that time, though only some of these are covered in Leng's 2008 *Katalog*, which nominally limits its scope to illustrated medieval manuscripts.

4 Note that Meyer's city of residence is today part of France and known as Strasbourg; in Meyer's day the city was German-speaking and known as Strassburg. Usage in this book reflects the distinction between modern Strasbourg and sixteenth-century Strassburg.

5 The typical age at first marriage in Strassburg at the time, early to mid-20s (Kintz, *La société strasbourgeoise*, p. 198), was in line with middle-class European norms of the day.

6 On sixteenth-century Strassburg, see Kintz, *La société strasbourgeoise*, pp. 235, 415–18; Châtelet-Lange, *Strasbourg en 1548*, p. 65.

7 On the Smiths, see Riff, 'La Corporation des Maréchaux'.

8 Kintz, *La société strasbourgeoise*, pp. 191–4.

9 On the life of artisans in Strassburg in the period, see Rott, 'Artisanat et mouvements sociaux'.
10 Solms-Laubach, *Geschichte*, p. 267.
11 On Stimmer, see Meyer, *Art of Combat*, p. 10; see also Beaujean and Tanner, *Stimmer*, pp. xiii, 71, 164–73; Bendel, *Stimmer*, pp. 52, 73–5; Kunstmuseum Basel, *Spätrenaissance*, p. 198; Nagler, *Künstler-Lexicon*, vol. 11, pp. 363–5; Nagler and Andresen, *Monogrammisten*, vol. 4, p. 519.
12 Kintz, *La société strasbourgeoise*, pp. 131 n. 2, 507; Livet and Rapp, *Histoire de Strasbourg*, vol. 2, p. 336.
13 The woodcuts may have reappeared in a subsequent seventeenth-century publication, *Künstlich und wolgerissene Fechters-Figuren und Stellungen, Geordnet durch Weyland den Kunstreichen und wolerfahrnen Jost Amman, Mahlern, von Zürych. Allen Künstlern, als Mahlern, Bildhauern, Goldschmiden, Steinmetzen, Schreinern &c. sehr nützlich* (Ulm: in Verlegung Mattheus Schultes, [c. 1680]). The work is referenced in Becker and Weigel, *Jobst Amman*, pp. 234–5, but a surviving copy has yet to be located.
14 Günterode, *De veris principiis*, sig. C3r–v; for the manuscript version of this text, see Dresden, Sächsische Landesbibliothek MS Dresd.C.15, fol. 17r. See Meyer, *Art of Combat*, pp. 10–11, for further discussion of this text.
15 Pacheco de Narváez, *Nueva ciencia*, sig. §5r, ¶¶3r, pp. 403, 490, 578, 657; Marcelli, *Regole della Scherma*, sig. B2r; Pallavicini, *La scherma illustrata*, p. 10. Marcelli and Pallavicini erroneously give Meyer's date of publication as 1568. By contrast, Narváez's references do correspond to Meyer's content, even if they may refer more to the images than the text; he also erroneously believes that Meyer's work is a translation of Marozzo (pp. 490, 578).
16 On the discrepancies in Pallavicini's references to Meyer, see Meyer, *Art of Combat*, p. 27 n. 5. In addition to known surviving works by Meyer, there is some evidence that could indicate a lost Meyer manuscript formerly in the Bavarian royal collection. Several nineteenth-century sources mention a manuscript with rich colour illustrations by Joachim Meyer dated 1561, displayed in the late 1800s

at the Royal Bavarian National Museum; the dedicatee is variously given as Hans Georg von Pfalz-Veldenz or Johann Pfalzgraf bei Rhein. Wilhelm Lübeck specifies that the manuscript included 'an illustration of an unusable sword, the crossbar of which is transformed into a warhammer and the pommel into a morning-star' (*Fechtkunst*, p. 6). But it seems improbable that Meyer had the means to produce a richly illuminated manuscript in 1561 when he had only just become a citizen of Strassburg, especially given that a decade later he struggled to finance his printed *Fechtbuch*. Aside from the date and dedication, the manuscript matches the description of the Latin version of Paulus Hector Mair's *Fechtbuch*, which has been in the Bavarian royal collection since 1567 (Munich, Bayerische Staatsbibliothek Cod. icon. 393; cf. fols. 230r ff. for the duelling sword). The manuscript could have been misattributed by confusion of name and other data; in any case, if an additional Meyer manuscript was in the Bavarian royal collection, it must be regarded as definitively lost, as this collection has been well combed over for such material. See *Führer durch das königlich Bayerische Nationalmuseum*, p. 102; Murray, *Handbook*, p. 75.

17 I am indebted to Heike Tröger of the Universitätsbibliothek Rostock for sharing her notes on the manuscript. I here designate the manuscript Meyer's Rostock Fechtbuch for convenience. Note that it is not the only *Fechtbuch* in the Rostock University Library: see Bauer, 'Hugold Behr.'

18 Rostock Fechtbuch, fols. 6r–39v, 41r–67r, 74v–75r, 98r–110r. On the various strands in the Liechtenauer commentaries, see Forgeng, 'Owning the Art', pp. 167–8; Forgeng and Kiermayer, 'The Chivalric Art', pp. 155–7. The Starhemberg manuscript (Rome, Biblioteca dell'Academica Nazionale dei Lincei e Corsiniana Cod. 44 A 8) is often named for Peter von Danzig, the last author who appears in the work, but this nomenclature is problematic, as I have explained elsewhere.

19 Rostock Fechtbuch, fols. 112r–121r. On Leckückner, see Forgeng, *Leckückner*; Forgeng, 'Owning the Art', p. 168; Forgeng and Kiermayer, 'The Chivalric Art', p. 157.

20 Rostock Fechtbuch, fols. 39v–41r, 67r–74v, 75v, 86r–v, 90r–98r. For translations of some of these texts, see Tobler, *Saint George*.
21 Rostock Fechtbuch, fols. 76r–86r, cf. Mair, *Fechtbuch* (Vienna), fols. 227r–246v.
22 Rostock Fechtbuch, fols. 123r–127r.
23 This dating may reflect a misinterpretation of the Swedish *1560-talet*, which means 'the 1560s,' not '1560'.
24 In 1566 at the Diet of Augsburg, Emperor Maximilian II granted the title of Academy to the Strassburg *Gymnasium*, with the right to grant the degrees of Bachelor and Master of Arts; the Academy would be further elevated to the status of University in 1621 (Strobel, *Histoire du gymnase protestant*, pp. 16, 24, 117–20; Livet and Rapp, *Histoire de Strasbourg*, vol. 2, pp. 448–9).
25 On Otto's biography, see Solms-Laubach, *Geschichte*, pp. 266–7; Walde, *Krigsbyten*, pp. 184–92.
26 Walde, *Krigsbyten*, pp. 181–3, 192–5.
27 Some of the ink numbers were altered in ink: for example, fol. 27 was originally numbered 18 in ink; this was altered in ink to 28, and finally renumbered 27 in pencil. Due to the trimming of the upper right-hand corners and consequent loss of many of the original folio numbers, it is impossible to offer a solid hypothesis as to the reason – it may again be a matter of error in the original numeration.
28 On the longsword, see Laking, *Record*, vol. 2, pp. 251–61; Müller and Kölling, *Hieb- und Stichwaffen*, pp. 168, 364; Meyer, *Art of Combat*, pp. 16–17; Seitz, *Blankwaffen*, vol. 1, pp. 134–5, 156–60, 281–99.
29 For some earlier illustrations of fencing longswords, see the Starhemberg Fechtbuch, fols. 1v–2v; Talhoffer, *Medieval Combat*, pl. 1–3; Mair, *Fechtbuch* (Vienna MS), fols. 1.1r ff. For later examples, see Thibault, *Académie*, vol. 2, pl. 9–11: p. 106.
30 For other surviving examples, see Blasco et al., *L'épée*, pp. 44–5, 50–1, 123 (cat. no. 48), 124 (cat. no. 51); Laking, *Record*, vol. 4, p. 270; LaRocca, *Academy*, p. 27; New Gallery, *Exhibition*, pp. 157–8, nos. 662, 663; Schneider and Stüber, *Waffen*, pp. 118–21; Wilczek, *Erinnerungen*, pl. 11 no. 1. Cf.

also the related tournament broadswords shown in Müller and Kölling, *Hieb- und Stichwaffen*, pp. 225, 382; and Dufty, *European Swords*, pl. 39a.

31 Cf. Boccia and Coelho, *Armi Bianche*, pp. 109–10, 122, 314–15; Laking, *Record*, vol. 4, pp. 270–2; LaRocca, 'Renaissance Spirit', p. 48; Oakeshott, *European Weapons*, p. 146.

32 On Liechtenauer's longsword verses and their legacy, see Forgeng, 'Owning the Art', pp. 167–8; Forgeng and Kiermayer, 'The Chivalric Art', pp. 155–7; Meyer, *Art of Combat*, pp. 11–12. Liechtenauer's verses are transcribed and translated in Tobler, *Saint George*, pp. 96–102.

33 Starhemberg Fechtbuch, fols. 37r–v; Tobler, *Saint George*, p. 130.

34 On the *langes Messer*, see Forgeng, *Lecküchner*, pp. xii–xvii. The typology of the dusack is complicated by the fact that the same name is often applied to a type of basket-hilted military saber of the same period (cf. Krenn, *Schwert und Spiess*, pp. 38–41; Krenn and Kamniker, 'Dusäggen'; Landeszeughaus, *Schwert und Säbel*, pp. 55–8 and pl. 5; Reichsstadtmuseum Rothenburg, *Katalog*, pp. 464–6; Seitz, *Blankwaffen*, vol. 1, pp. 359–64).

35 On the dusack, see Amberger, *Secret History*, pp. 113–19, 222–3; Anon., 'Dusaken'; Boeheim, *Waffenkunde*, pp. 273–4; Deutsches Klingenmuseum Solingen, *Klingenmuseum*, p. 100; Grimm and Grimm, *Wörterbuch*, s.v. Disak; Krenn and Kamniker, 'Dusäggen', p. 139 and nn. 6–9; Landeszeughaus, *Schwert und Säbel*, p. 55; Meyer, *Art of Combat*, p. 17; Seitz, *Blankwaffen*, vol. 1, pp. 266–7, 360–3. On the material from which it was made, cf. also Wassmannsdorff, *Fechtschulen*, pp. 12, 14; Mair, *Fechtbuch* (Vienna MS), 1.97r ff. A few metal examples are known, but these seem to have been extremely rare, and have not been adequately studied (cf. Boeheim, *Waffenkunde*, p. 273; Demmin, *Weapons*, p. 379; Demmin, *Kriegswaffen*, pp. 726–8; Dolínek and Durdík, *Encyclopedia*, p. 89; Reichsstadtmuseum Rothenburg, *Katalog*, p. 497).

36 For example, Mair, *Fechtbuch* (Vienna MS), fols. 1.97r ff.

37 On Leckúchner, see Forgeng, *Leckúchner*; Forgeng, 'Owning the Art', p. 168; Forgeng and Kiermayer, 'The Chivalric Art', p. 157.

38 Paurenfeindt, *Fechterey*, sigs. G2r–I1r.

39 Mair, *Fechtbuch* (Vienna MS) 1.97r–118v.

40 Meyer, *Art of Combat*, 2.50r.

41 On the rapier, see Capwell, *Noble Art*; LaRocca, 'Renaissance Spirit'; Meyer, *Art of Combat*, pp. 19–20; Müller and Kölling, *Hieb- und Stichwaffen*, pp. 69–75; Norman, *Rapier and Smallsword*; North, 'Rapier to Smallsword'; Seitz, *Blankwaffen*, vol. 1, pp. 303–39.

42 For surviving versions of fencing rapiers, cf. Florence, Museo Nazionale del Bargello C1675 and BD695 (Boccia and Coelho, *Armi Bianche*, figs. 533–4; Capwell, *Noble Art*, p. 139 fn. 88); Leeds, Royal Armouries Museum IX.120 (Capwell, *Noble Art*, pp. 121–3); Victoria and Albert Museum M.2749-1931 (Capwell, *Noble Art*, pp. 122–3, 139 fn. 88).

Joachim Meyer's

Art of Sword Combat

<2r>

<2v–3r blank; 3v>

<4r, A-hand begins>

[Preface]

To the well-born lord, Lord Otto Count von Solms, lord of Münzenberg and Sonnenwalde etc., my gracious lord:

Well-born gracious lord, may my humble willing service be at all time present to your Grace. Gracious lord, ancient authors diligently praised and extolled the chivalric liberal art of combat in their books, instilling and earnestly commending it for princes and lords, and with good reason, particularly since we read in credible sources that it was the basis for most chivalric duelling and excellent deeds. For not only do Greek and Roman historians show what virility arose from it through excellent courage, and what glory has been attained through it in the highest leadership and supervision of warfare, but also daily experience demonstrates that whoever practises and diligently studies knightly sports and combat <*4v*> greatly outdoes those who have not practised, and skilfully outshines them in all things.

Therefore in our own times princes and lords greatly love and promote this art, no less than our ancestors; and your Grace has also earnestly embraced this virile art along with other liberal arts, and has summoned me to it as an honest combat-master to instruct your Grace in this art; and I have undertaken this in all humility with willing spirit. Since I have not only found a particular charm in this art, but also your Grace's gracious and well-disposed will toward me, I have not spared in any way to humbly serve your Grace in this art.

Therefore I present your Grace this compiled Combat-Book with all its techniques, in the humble hope that your Grace will not only retain in mind the techniques that you have learned by reading about them, but also may learn from it many skills and useful *<5r>* techniques, no less than when your Grace had a daily combat-master with you. I therefore humbly pray your Grace will graciously receive this work of mine, however worthless and paltry it may be, as it flows from a heart humble and well-meaning toward your Grace in all possible service. I wish to be most diligent in this so that I may humbly serve and please your Grace.

May Almighty God grant your Grace long life in health and peace along with other benefits etc.

Your Grace's humble and willing
Joachim Meyer
Combat-Master [*Fechtmeister*]

<5v blank; one folio apparently missing here; 6r>

Sword Combat

First, every attack combination in combat is divided into three stages which you should particularly observe in the sword, namely the attack, the followup, and the withdrawal or ending. Thus first, in the approach, the attack happens through the guards and cuts as they will follow hereafter; then in the second part and middle-work one follows up with the handwork and combinations of suitable cuts; and lastly comes the ending or withdrawal. And each of these will be diligently described and taught in orderly fashion hereafter in its place.

Secondly, you shall take heed of the Before and After, foible and forte. The Before is when you drive your opponent with your techniques so that he cannot achieve his intent, but confines himself to parrying, to defend against your techniques and counter and bar them, so that he leaves the Before to you.

The After is when you are rushed upon by your opponent as has just been described, then you shall instantly counter him quickly with suitable work, so that you impede him in his techniques, and so with your work deprive him of the Before, forcing him to parry you in the After. Thus there is a stubborn exchange with the Before and After, so that now one of you has it, now the other. Anyone who does not pay heed to it will never learn to do anything sure in combat.

<*6v*>

Division of the Sword into Foible and Forte

The sword is divided firstly into two parts, namely from the haft to the middle of the blade, which is the forte, then the middle to the tip is the foible.

The sword is further divided into four parts as the illustration below indicates. The nearer part, that is the haft, encompasses the work with the pommel along with the crossbar and grip. Next, the second part encompasses the work with slicing and pressing and whatever pertains to the forte. With the third part of the sword you should note the changing work of the foible and forte according to opportunity and will. The furthermost part pertains only to the foible with working to the opening.

Hard and Soft

Note that in the bindings of the sword, you will feel whether he has bound hard or soft with the cut, and whether he is strong or soft in holding against you. And you commonly have to guard more against soft than strong binds, as will be seen hereafter in the section on combat.

And so that the sword combat and techniques described hereafter may be more comprehensible, I will explain in my following epitome how I would have the terms understood according to the aforementioned order, namely beginning, middle, and end.

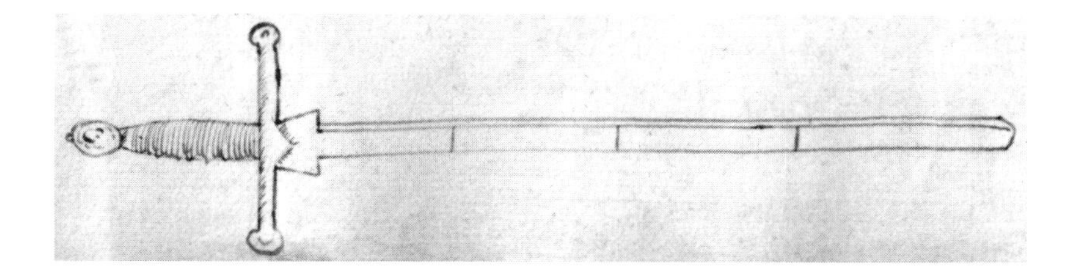

<7r>

Here Follows the Epitome of Sword Combat

The Four Chief Guards
'From the Day' [*Von Dach*]
Fool [*Olber*]
Ox [*Ochs*]
Plow [*Pflug*]

The Eight Secondary Guards
Longpoint [*Langort*]
Irongate [*Eysenport*]
Hanging Point [*Hengetort*]
Speaking-Window [*Sprechfenster*]
Key [*Schlüssel*]
Side Guard [*Nebenhuot*]
Crossed Guard [*Schranckhut*]
Wrath Guard [*Zornleger*]

The Five Master Cuts
Wrath Cut [*Zornhaw*]
Crooked Cut [*Krumphaw*]
Thwart Cut [*Zwerchhaw*]
Squinter Cut [*Schylerhaw*]
Scalper [*Scheideler*]

The Six Secret Cuts
Blind Cut [*Blindthaw*]
Rebound Cut [*Brellhaw*]
Short Cut [*Kurtzhaw*]
Wrist Cut [*Knuchellhaw*]

Clashing Cut [*Glützhaw*]
Winding Cut [*Windthaw*]

Handwork in the Sword
Binding [*Anbinden*]
Remaining [*Bleiben*]
Slicing [*Schneiden*]
Striking around [*Umbschlagen*]
Chasing [*Nachreisen*]
Snapping around [*Umbschnappen*]
Running off [*Ablauffen*]
Doubling [*Doplieren*]
Deceiving [*Verfurenn*]
Flitting [*Verfligen*]
Failing [*Verfelen*]
Circle [*Zyrckel*]
Loop [*Rinde*]
Winding [*Winden*]
Winding through [*Durchwinden*]
Reversing [*Verkeren*]
Changing through [*Durchwechslen*]
Overrunning [*Überlauffen*]
Setting off [*Absetzen*]
Slicing off [*Abschneiden*]
Pulling [*Zucken*]
Pressing hands [*Hendttrucken*]
Sliding [*Verscheiben*]
Hanging [*Verhengen*]
Blocking [*Verstillen*]
Barring [*Sperren*]
Wrenching [*Aussreissen*]
Gripping over [*Übergreiffen*]
Seizing the foible [*Schwech fassen*]

<7v>

Concerning the Four Openings and Division of the Combatant

Space has been left on this page for an illustration, demarcated with scribed lines, but it was never executed. This space was evidently intended for an illustration of target areas, as referenced on this folio and fol. 44v; its equivalent is here supplied from Meyer's published woodcuts. Note that this illustration has a second horizontal line across the face, referenced in the published book but not in this manuscript.
Worcester Art Museum (MA), The John Woodman Higgins Collection, 2014.583.

Firstly, the combatant is divided into two sides, namely left and right, as shown by the vertical line in the illustration; then into two parts, namely the lower and upper; the upper two openings are assigned to the Ox, the lower ones to the Plow. Use them as follows: first, notice in which part he holds his sword, below or above, to the right or left. When you have seen this, then at once attack opposite, whether diagonally or otherwise. Here is an example:

> In the onset when you both come together and you see that he holds his sword in his upper right part, whether it is in the Ox or Wrath Cut, then attack him in his left lower opening, not with the intent to hit, but rather to incite him to meet you; as soon as it clashes or touches, then pull around your head and strike above to the opening from which he has come, namely to his right ear, with the half edge and crossed hands; <*8r*> that is the true Squinter Cut. **7r.1**

Another

> In the onset when the opponent holds his sword on the left, then go through before him from your right, and cut with strength to his right. As soon as he slips after the strike, then pull in a loop to the left opening; if he slips after it again, then let it fly back around, thus going from one opening to the other, crosswise and opposite to each other according to opportunity. **8r.1**

Every fighter should be promptly heedful in all hits, from whichever opening the cut has come, instantly to pursue there.

And before concluding I will add the teaching concerning parrying. It is written in the old epitomes, 'Who often parries is often hit.'[1] Item, Liechtenauer says in his secret words, 'Guard yourself against parrying, if need befalls you it will tire you.'[2] Therefore every fighter should be accustomed to be the first to attack and finish, for if a fighter watches and waits for his opponent, he rarely comes away without shame, or at the very least he does not achieve much. A true fighter does not parry much unless there is some great advantage: 'And when the opponent strikes so he strikes too; if the opponent thrusts then he thrusts too; if the opponent steps, he steps also.'[3] For when two matched strokes come together, they bring their <*8v*> parrying with them; and when someone cuts from above and you cut against it with a Thwart, then you parry and hit at the same time. Likewise you shall pay attention to simultaneous cutting and take good heed of your advantage in it. Therefore every fighter should be promptly heedful as has been said above, for when two good fighters come together, whoever thinks quicker triumphs quicker.

Thus I have presented sword combat and all needful techniques in brief and summary form, and also somewhat explained the rather obscure terms, and afterwards integrated them into an attack combination, dividing it into three parts, namely (as I said initially)

---

1 Cf. this passage to Meyer, *Art of Combat*, 1.15v–16r.

2 Liechtenauer, 'Merktext', ll. 133–4; Tobler, *Saint George*, p. 100.

3 Cf. the Ringeck Fechtbuch, fol. 35r: 'When he cuts, then cut too, and when he thrusts, then thrust too.'

the beginning or attack, the followup or middle-work, and last the withdrawal or end. So that you may understand it better I will reiterate it briefly, as follows: for the attack I have presented the guards, in which you should not tarry and wait, but through which you should attack to the uttermost with one or two of the cuts I have described, according to opportunity. Now when you have attacked and the Before has run off from you, then in the second part you shall follow up with all kinds of proper handwork, to hold onto the Before; this handwork also is presented above. Thirdly you should crowd and confine him with handwork so that you can come to the withdrawal without harm. *<9r>*

I will give an example of this:

> When someone fights against you from the Day Guard, then if you come in the onset into the Side Guard, you shall not wait there longer than until he pulls up his sword for the stroke; as soon as he brings his sword up in the air, meet him with a Thwart Blow; the instant it clashes, cut quickly back around with a long Thwart to the other side on his sword; now you have executed the attack. If he strikes around, then slice after him; if he parries, deceive him; if he escapes, chase him; if he is hard, be soft; if he strikes, counter it; if he parries, strike. Thirdly also pay attention instantly for your opportunity for the withdrawal etc. **9r.1** **1.26r.1**

<9v blank; B-hand begins>

[Longsword Verses]

<10r>

> See that you are the first on the field;
> before your opponent adopts a guard, lay on against him. [*1570 ll. 29–30*]

Note this as follows: when you wish to fight with someone, see that you are the first to be in place, so that you can act in a timely manner with your intended techniques; then you should at once proceed to execute cuts, not letting him adopt a guard or technique at his will; rather you should rush upon him with secret steps before he realises it, as will be further explained in the following verses.

> Pay heed to Instantly, understand me rightly,
> hit him before he adopts his guard. [*1570 ll. 31–2*]

That is, when you are in the onset, take heed when he is almost in range of you, and the moment he acts as if he will adopt a guard, do not let him be in peace or come to it, but always attack through before him; and as he is choosing a guard, lay on at once to the nearest opening; and act as if you intended to cut strongly, but don't do this, rather let it run off without hitting, or flit to another opening; then as soon as you are halfway in with your blade *<10v>* or have come onto his sword, then do not be idle, but deliver a Thwart, strike around, wrench, slice, wind, or do whatever work may arise for you.

> No guard comes to you that is so good;
> in the After you will hit him with free mettle. [*1570 ll. 33–4*]

Now you might say, 'What do you mean? – there are so many good guards, and also you yourself have taught how to execute many good techniques from them.' The answer: it is true, there are many good guards, and fine and good techniques can be executed from the various guards, as I have presented some of them to you in this book. Yet these verses teach that it is always better not to settle fully into a guard, since from the guards someone can easily see what you mean to execute against him, something that cannot be seen so well from the cuts.

Also these verses teach you how to act against him in the After, that is, how you shall hit him in the After: when he positions himself or stands in a guard, cut opposite it to the other opening; as soon as he goes out of his guard against the cut to take your cut with parrying, then pull back around your head just as it connects, or before it connects at all, and strike in at the very same part or quarter from which he has gone away. <*11r*>

I will offer you an example of this:

11r.1
1.46r.1

In the onset, if your opponent stands before you in the right Wrath Guard, as soon as you see that he adopts the Wrath Guard, cut through before him, but such that you are not too near him; and in cutting through, let your sword fly in the air, as if you intended to come into the right Ox. But just at the moment you show this or have positioned yourself as if you were about to do it, step quickly just as he perceives it and cut in from below at his left, such that your hands are high. Thus you force him either to come out of his guard to parry you, or to cut in at the same time with a back-step. If he cuts, then as soon as the swords connect, pull around your head, and deliver a Squinting Cut at his right ear in a single fluid action with crossed hands as he goes away to the opening, as the illustration shows.[4] This is a very fine attack or fight, in which you shall pay good heed to the stepping, and let your body fully follow the cut.

When you threaten to strike to a place, you can very readily deceive an opponent. To do this, you must as it were steal the ground from him in laying on, and in the approach, act as if you were going to take a small and tight step; then before he knows it, step broadly to the attack. Contrarily, first act as if you intend to step broadly: when your opponent perceives this, and hastily tries to meet you in earnest to get there before you, restrain your step, and do it moderately, so that he wears himself out for nothing. Meanwhile look for your advantage, and as soon as you see it you should be rapidly back upon him with broad stepping.

<11v>

Send your cuts powerfully from your body,
carry out your work to the four openings. [*1570 ll. 35–6*]

---

4 See Image 1. The published *Art of Combat* here references Image G, though none of the images in the woodcut is a good match for the Lund illustration, or for the 1570 text. The closest matches to the Lund illustration are in woodcuts L and B.

This verse covers two things, first concerning the cuts, second concerning the four parts of the opponent to which the cuts are delivered. And note that you should deliver all cuts with outstretched arms, and also extend well to the opponent; and as soon as a cut misses on one side, you shall swiftly cut opposite to it from the other side. Item, if you should hit and are blocked, then swiftly strike around to the other side. Also, when you mean to cut to an opening, the moment he encounters your cut to parry it, then (if you can) do not let it touch, but pull your sword back away flying freely, and let the stroke fly back into another opening. When you thus extend well from you with the cuts and do the steps correctly with them, no changing or changing through can come onto your shield or harm you, as long as you cut to the body and not to the sword.

Concerning the second line of this verse you have been instructed in the first section, and I will write further about it in the 38th verse,[5] and will refrain from writing more about it here.

> When you deliver a Crooked Cut, go up quickly,
> cast the point crosswise on his hands. [*1570 ll. 37–8*]

Note that the Crooked Cuts take many forms, for all cuts that are delivered with crossed hands are called Crooked Cuts; *<12r>* thus the one Squinter is also reckoned among the Crooked Cuts – for it doesn't matter whether they are done with the full or the half edge, as long as you hold your hands crosswise.

---

5 i.e. ll. 69–70, fol. 25v.

12r.1
1.47r.1

And firstly note: when an opponent cuts at your head straight down from his right, step with your right foot well out from his stroke towards his left, so that you escape his stroke as it were in a spring towards his left side, and cut with crossed hands from your right against his cut; thus your blade comes between his head and sword onto his half edge, which is facing him. As soon as it connects, step further with your right foot around to his left side and displace or transfer your blade from his blade down onto his arm, between his head and sword.[6] Meanwhile you will surely find an opening to which you may cut, and you should not delay long, but let it quickly fly to the opening.

12r.2
1.47v.1

Item, note: in the onset when you come to your opponent, see when he pulls his arms up for the stroke, and cross your hands in the air, such that they remain high,[7] and cast the point (that is, the foible or furthest part of your blade) onto his hands or arms. This shall take place as he draws up for the stroke, and before he is ready you shall already be back on his blade with a Thwart, for these techniques shall take place fluidly and quickly.

<12v: Image 1; 13r>

Let the Circle connect,[8]
hold your hands high, if you wish to deceive him.
[*1570 ll. 39–40*]

---

6 1570 adds *Push his arm down thus with crossed hands with a jerk.*
7 *such that they remain high*] not in 1570.
8 1570 adds *to the right.*

The Circle also comes from the Crooked Cuts, and is a particularly good technique for deceiving compared to others, since it does not run off without connecting (as do other deceiving techniques, like running off[9] and such); but if you do it rightly, the Circle hits very hard with the half edge as it runs by. Execute this technique as follows:

> After you have come under his sword with the attack, and you stand before your opponent in the bind, sending your sword up above your head, as soon as he allows you space and does not bind after your sword, but also sends his sword-point high, then cross your hands in the air, and cut down from above at his right ear in this crossed position with the short edge, so that, whether it hits or not, your blade runs around past beside his right arm in a Circle; and meanwhile keep your hands up over your head. As soon as he slips after the Circle, then step with your left foot well out to his right side, and cut at his head with the long edge behind his blade over his right arm; take your body[10] well out from his stroke on your left side as you step.

13r.1
1.47v.2

<13v>

A Good Technique with the Circle

> When you stand in this sort of work before your opponent (as I have already taught), then take heed when the opportunity comes to you, and step sideways with your left foot out to your left side, and

13v.1
1.47v.3

---

9 1570 adds *flitting*.
10 1570 adds *and head*.

cut a Circle past at his right as you step, but such that in running past to the right it grazes.[11] And with this Circle, step through with your right foot between you and him to his right side; and as you step through, deliver a Thwart Cut from your right at his left, forwards at his face;[12] instantly spring well out to his right, and cut long after at his head.

Step well with the Crooked if you wish to parry;
the crossing over will do him harm. [*1570 ll. 45–6*]

That is, when you cut in with the Crooked at the same time as him, then as you cut, step well out from his stroke, so that you have your head out from his stroke behind your blade. The second part teaches that when you bind with a Crooked Cut on his sword you should quickly cross over (if you have the opportunity), at once snap around, or wind the flickings [at his head],[13] or wrench, let it overrun.

<14r: Image 2; 14v>

A Technique from the Reverser

14v.1
1.48v.1
Note, in the onset, when your opponent goes up before you, step and deliver a Crooked Cut[14] to or over his right arm; with this Crooked Cut, step well to him, and reverse your sword, and wrench

11 1570 adds *and hits.*
12 1570 here references Image K.
13 *at his head*] *noch* ~~*dhan*~~ *schnap kopf*; 1570 *nach seinem kopf*. The text has been corrupted here by dittography from the previous line.
14 1570 adds *from your left with the short edge and crossed hands.*

downwards to your right side. If he works upwards with his arms so that you cannot force him down, then send your pommel between his arms from inside; release your left hand from the haft, grip your blade, and wrench upwards as this image shows you.[15]

Counter: release your left hand and let him wrench in vain; instantly pursue his jerking upwards with the slice on his arm; do not let him come to any further work or get free, until you see your opportunity; at once let your weapon fly to the next opening. **14v.2** **1.48v.2**

Crooked to the flat,
if you wish to weaken the masters.[16] [*1570 ll. 47–8*]

This teaches how you shall weaken your opponent's incoming stroke. Do it as follows:

In the onset, take heed when he cuts at you from his right, and step well out from his stroke, and cut with crossed hands and the long edge onto the forte **14v.3** **1.48v.3**

<15r: Image 3; 15v>

of his blade in the flat; thus you weaken him so that he can scarcely recover for another stroke; then

15 See Image 3; the image illustrates the reversing and wrench described earlier in the technique. The 1570 text references Image O, but it is a very different image from the one here.

16 1570 text is different for these verses; the version here is closer to the equivalent lines in Liechtenauer ('Merktext,' ll. 80–1; Tobler, *Saint George*, p. 98).

before he recovers, you can be on his head with winding or flicking.

15v.1
1.49v.1

Counter: if you see that an opponent meets you with a Crooked Cut on your incoming stroke to weaken you, then quickly change through under his blade, and work to the side from which he has delivered the Crooked Cut.

As soon as it connects and clashes above,
pull away to the opening if you wish to confuse him.
[*1570 ll. 49–50*]

This is a very good verse, which admonishes you seriously to pay heed to the opening that appears. For if you pursue the matter correctly, it is certain that whenever two strokes connect or clash together above, you will have an opening below: this will not fail you. Observe this through some techniques, as follows:

15v.2
1.49v.2

Note, in the onset, position yourself in the Wrath Guard;[17] as soon as you think you can reach your opponent, step and deliver a powerful High Cut with him in from your right. As soon as it clashes, quickly strike around again with a Thwart[18] to his left ear, with a back-step on your left foot behind your right.[19] Thus you hit him twice, as it were, or complete two strokes on one side before he gets one.

---

17 *position yourself in the Wrath Guard*] not in 1570.
18 *with a Thwart*] not in 1570.
19 *with a back-step … right*] 1570 *and at the same time step with your left foot behind your right.*

<16r>

Item, if an opponent cuts at you from above as before, then cut from your left from below against his stroke, so that you catch his High Cut up in the air.[20] As soon as it clashes, cut[21] with the short-edge foible with crossed hands, in a Circle at his right ear. And this shall take place swiftly, almost at the same time, namely that when the blades connect, the half edge will at once hit down from above. **16r.1** **1.49v.3**

In the onset, act as if you intended to cut from above; as soon as you see that he slips up against the cut, at once turn your High Cut into a Low Cut before it actually connects above; this is like a Failer.[22] **16r.2** **1.49v.4**

Item, if he cuts from below, fall on it from above with your long edge. As soon as it clashes, pull quickly away and strike to the nearest opening in a single motion, or strike around from his sword with the flat in a flick that you wind to the nearest opening. **16r.3** **1.49v.5**

When you cut crooked to the forte,
be sure to wind through and overrun with it. [*1570 ll. 41–2*]

That is, when you deliver a Crooked Cut at an opponent, and he opposes hard against it so that you cannot get him above with crossing over or other work, then **16r.4** **1.50r.1**

20 1570 adds *with crossed hands.*
21 1570 adds *off of his sword.*
22 1570 adds *and you thus hit his left ear before he realises it.*

<16v: Image 4; 17r>

wind through below with the pommel, and use it to catch over his blade or arm outside on the other side, and wrench down; strike him on his head with the long edge as you wrench; or catch with the pommel between his hands, as this illustration shows.[23]

17r.1
1.50r.2 The second is a counter to a Low Cut, as follows:[24] if an opponent delivers a Low Cut at you, then cut above on his forte with your long edge so that you have your hands crooked or crosswise. As soon as it clashes, shoot the blade right in before you and, in thrusting forth, wind the short edge to flick it around at his face or head. If he goes up and wards off the flick, then go up also, and pull around your head, and strike to another opening.

You should pay heed to the deceit of the pommel,
with the Tag-Hit and flicking you will vex him. [*1570 ll. 43–4*]

17r.2
1.50r.3 That is, when you cut in with a Crooked Cut at his forte,[25] and he opposes or parries high, then wind through below with the pommel, and act as if you intended to catch over with the pommel, as I have already taught; and before he realises it, flick the

23 See Image 4. 1570 references Image O. Compare also the version of this technique in the Ringeck Fechtbuch, fol. 35v.
24 *The second is … follows*] 1570 *Counter*. Here the manuscript makes more sense than the published version, which seems to be presented as a counter to the previous technique, rather than to a Low Cut.
25 *forte*] 1570 *right*.

short edge back in at him, to whichever side you first did the Crooked Cut.

Item, in the onset, lay on against your opponent with a powerful horizontal Middle Cut strongly at his left ear. Quickly pull your pommel around your head, and threaten him with it as if you intended to jab at his other side with the pommel; when he slips against it to parry the jab, <*17v*> flick back at his left ear with the short edge, and as you flick, step with your left foot back behind your right.[26] **17r.3** **1.50r.4**

Also if you wish to shoot through correctly,
Crooked, Short, change through on his shield. [*1570 ll. 51–2*]

This is a true little master technique: when you are in the onset, position yourself in the right Wrath; as soon as he brings his sword into the air, deliver a free High Cut at him; and[27] cross your sword[28] in the air, so that the right hand comes crosswise over the left, and thus deftly cut through crooked with the short edge against his cut. Instantly double step well out to his right, and cut with the long edge at his right ear, or use changing through to come onto his shield against his right; thus work with winding, slicing, and whatever work arises for you. **17v.1** **1.50v.1**

26 1570 adds *and cut away from him.*
27 *and*] 1570 *but do not complete it, instead.*
28 *sword*] 1570 *hands.*

A Free-Running Technique from Shooting Through

17v.2
1.50v.2

Take heed in the onset as your opponent pulls up his sword for the stroke, and cut through crooked quickly and deftly before him (as I have taught above) so that you come to his right on his shield. As soon as it connects, wind the short edge [inwards][29] at his head, and, in this winding, jerk your pommel well upwards, so that the short edge comes deep. If he goes and parries, let your blade snap around again so that your hands come crosswise, the right over the left; flick thus with crossed hands; in snapping around, wind[30] in below at his right ear; and meanwhile step with your left foot well out to his right as you flick. Then at once deliver a Thwart back around deep at his left ear with a back-step, and wind your short edge on his sword inwards and[31] back out at his left ear, and cut away from him.

<18r>

Note when he will confuse you with the Crooked,
remain rightly on the sword; carry out the War
with winding, slicing, and everything else;
with flitting let yourself not go too far. [*1570 ll. 53–6*]

These verses teach you how to conduct yourself against an opponent who binds you crooked on your sword. And it properly speaks of two elements, namely remaining and the War. That is, when someone binds

29 *inwards*] *entweders;* 1570 *einwerts.*
30 *wind*] 1570 *flick back.*
31 *inwards and*] not in 1570.

you crooked on your sword, you should not pull away at once, but remain on his sword to feel what kind of work you will need; for example, if he withdraws, that you chase; or if he remains, that you wind.

For winding and slicing, wrenching, reversing, is called the War, through which you constantly counter the opponent's techniques. And one counter follows from another; for if he wards off one, then he gives you occasion or helps you to another technique that properly follows; and thus you both make war over it.[32] Therefore note: when an opponent lays on against you with a Crooked Cut, do not flit from one opening to another; for as soon as you go away from the Crooked Cut, then you are quite open to him, if he acts correctly.

Technique

> If someone delivers a Crooked Cut at you from his right, set off his cut upwards with the long edge, and when it clashes, remain with the bind on his blade; meanwhile wind your pommel up towards your left, and the blade down towards his left, the short edge at his left ear; and all this shall take place at the same time.[33] Thus you will certainly hit; but if he should be shrewd enough to turn the Crooked Cut into the Longpoint, then

18r.1
1.51r.1

<18v: Image 5; 19r>

32 *it*] 1570 *the Before.*
33 1570 adds *as one step.*

wind the short edge inwards at his head in a flick; at once wind back through again underneath with the pommel on your left side; thus catch over his blade or arm with the pommel, and wrench, or, depending on your situation, undertake some other technique as seems fitting to you.

Quickly flick the foible at the right,
doubly flick, protect yourself with the shield. [*1570 ll. 57–8*]

19r.1
1.51r.2

Note: in the onset, come into the right Change; from there, slash up through his face, so that your sword runs around in a loop over your head; step with your left foot well to his right, and strike with the outside flat from your left against his right across at his ear; with this, take your head well out of the way as illustrated above.[34] When it clashes, quickly push your pommel through under your right arm and flick with the inside flat up from below in a flicking around.[35] In this flicking around,[36] remain hard on his shield with your sword, and press hard from you. If he resists, let your sword go away without resisting him, pull around your head, and strike a strong Clashing Cut with the outside flat and overhand at his left;[37] let your pommel go back through under your arm, and flick from inside behind his blade at his head. Remain hard on his shield and wind rapidly

34 See Image 5.
35 *in a flicking around*] 1570 *back at his right ear.*
36 *flicking around*] 1570 *winding.*
37 1570 adds *so that your pommel goes well upwards; thus the cut goes that much deeper.*

back out; thus you stand back in the Clashing Cut as before. Work further as you will to the four openings, as you have been taught to do already.

Item, if your opponent delivers a High Cut at you from his right, then likewise deliver a High Cut in against his at the same time. When it clashes, rapidly push your pommel through under your arm, and flick back inwards at his head; just as it connects, pull your crossed arms up towards your left, and force upwards around on his blade; [flick back with the outside or back of your hand at his left ear from below],[38] as in the previous technique. This double flicking shall happen quickly, and <*19v*> I have presented it to you so particularly since it is an especially shrewd technique.

19r.2
1.51v.1

For if you bind from one side on his sword, and remain hard on it, and wind at him in and outwards in a flick, doubly on one side to the upper and lower part of his head, when he parries the flick, you will certainly have an opening on the other side that you may hit with a Circle, or by flicking around in a single motion.[39]

Also wind strongly against his shield,
instantly shove him away and strike swiftly. [*1570 ll. 59–60*]

---

38 *flick back … below*] The sense is here clarified by 1570; Lund *or back of the hand back at his left ear from below, and flick thus back with the outside.*
39 1570 adds *In my opinion you can well observe and learn the windings from this.*

19v.1
1.51v.2

That is, when an opponent wards off your double flicking, and sets you off, catch his shield with yours,[40] and push his sword away from you sideways. Instantly let your short edge snap around deep at his other opening on the opposite side.

19v.2
1.52v.1

If a powerful brute cuts at you, so that you cannot come at him with such subtle work, then cut the first at the same time as him, and just as he pulls his arms back towards him, go at him from underneath with horizontal blade on his arms; and in going under, release your left hand from the pommel and grip your blade in the middle, as shown by the following illustration.[41] Wrench his arms to the side with your shield and crossbar, and as you shove or wrench, release your left hand; quickly cut after, either short or long.

Therefore note, when you encounter a brute who is always cutting 'from the Day', then see that you parry him one stroke or two, until you see the opportunity. When he has gone up the furthest for a stroke, go quickly under his stroke onto his arms, and step well under him; thus he will strike his own arms on your blade.

<20r: Image 6; 20v>

The Squinting Cut you shall execute wisely,
with winding you can also double against him. [*1570 ll. 61–2*]

40 Cf. 1570 Image I.
41 See Image 6. 1570 references Image N.

There are three Squinters, namely two Squinting Cuts, one from the right, the second from your left, with crossed hands not unlike the Crooked Cut, as described above concerning the Crooked Cut. The third is a Squinter with the face, as when I look at a place, and act as if I intended to strike there, but I don't do this, but strike in somewhere else.

Do the first Squinting Cut as follows. When you are in the onset, then note as soon as he goes up for the stroke, to strike against your left, and position yourself as if you mean to strike in together with him; but don't do it, rather turn your sword in the air so that your hands come crosswise, and cut with crossed arms and the half edge together with him from above in against his right, so that his blade also comes against his right, or goes without hitting beside your right, and step well with your left foot on his right side.[42] **20v.1**

The second is the Old Squinting Cut, do it as follows:

In the onset, position yourself in the right Wrath Guard; if he cuts above to your head, then step and cut from your right against his cut with turned short edge over his sword to his head with outstretched arms, as the following illustration shows.[43] **20v.2**

---

42 This paragraph not in 1570.

43 See Image 7. This paragraph not in 1570. Instead of these two paragraphs, 1570 reads *You have already been taught about these Squinting Cuts in the first part, and since I speak of them here and there in the techniques, it is needless to discuss them more fully. I will therefore only say something of a few counters and the like that arise from them.*

<21r>

21r.1
1.52v.2
Note, when someone does a Squinting Cut against your long cut, he opens his right side; therefore do not let him come onto your sword, but change through beneath, and in going through cut at his right long in from your left.

21r.2
1.53r.1
Item, if someone changes through to your right side under your Squinting Cut, then remain with the point straight before his face, and turn the long edge against his sword; instantly let your pommel go through under your right arm, and step with your left foot well to his right side. Thus he has changed through in vain, for you come at his head with the first Squinting Cut with crossed hands. At once let it run off by his right side using the Circle, and deliver a Thwart at his left.[44]

Counter against the Plow

21r.3
1.53r.2
Note, when someone comes before you in the guard of the Plow, promptly lay on against him with the Squinting Cut.[45] As soon as he goes up, then work to his lower openings, and then to all four targets.

---

44 1570 adds *ear*.

45 A classic precept of the Liechtenauer tradition; cf. the Ringeck Fechtbuch, fol. 35r, Starhemberg Fechtbuch, fol. 26v (Tobler, *Saint George*, p. 122).

Counter against the Longpoint

Item, if someone stands before you in the Longpoint, act as if you intended to deliver a long High Cut at his left ear; don't do this, but turn around in the air, and deliver a strong Squinting Cut on his sword. As soon as it clashes, thrust the point in before you at his face; **21r.4** **1.53r.3**

<21v: Image 7; 22r>

he must parry this: as soon as he goes up, pull your sword around your head in a single motion; cut with the short edge and crossed hands horizontally at his right ear.[46] Let your left hand go well up under your right arm; thus the short edge goes deep. Pull back around your head, and wrench his blade across with the flat from your right against his left, so that your sword flies back around over your head, and let your short edge shoot in deep at his left ear. At once deliver two Low Cuts at his right and left; instantly cut away.

Item, if an opponent comes before you who likes to bind long on you from above, or sends his first stroke long at you from the Day, then when you are near him or come to him, slash through before him up towards your left, so that your blade shoots around over your head into the Plunge against his left.[47] Let your sword instantly snap around back over your head, the right hand over the left, and strike in at his **22r.1** **1.53v.1**

46 1570 adds *I call this the other Squinter.*

47 1570 adds *Menace him as if you intended thus to strike at his left; thus he will doubtless be prompt to cut in.*

right ear with the short edge at the same time as his stroke, as I have taught above. If you do this correctly and step well with it, then you will certainly hit, for the technique has often worked for me.[48] But if he parries and goes up (for he must go up if he wants to parry), at once pull around your head, and cut in with the long edge from below across at the radius-bone of his left forearm, close to his pommel at the wrist-bone. One of these two openings will come to you.[49] Pull your hilt back up around your <*22v*> head, and deliver a strong long cut at his left over his head; in this third stroke, step with both feet in a double step well around his left side; thus the cut works well. This is a good earnest technique, if you want to bring it home to the opponent.

Another Technique with the Squinting Cut

22v.1
1.53v.2

In the onset when you are almost in range of him, act as if you intended to deliver a long strong High Cut; when he goes up to meet you, turn the short edge in the air from your right against his left, and jerk your pommel upwards; strike him with the short edge over his arm or hands; step well to his left side. Let it run around past in a Circle, and cut long after at his nearest opening, or attack him with Low Cuts.

Doubling the Squinter

22v.2
1.54r.1

Item, in the approach deliver a Squinting Cut from your right against his cut on his sword. As soon as it

48 *for the technique … me*] not in 1570.
49 1570 adds *either the right ear or the radius.*

clashes, reverse your sword on his blade, and slip out on his blade towards your left side; step with your right foot further towards his left; let your blade go around your head, and deliver the second Squinting Cut to his head,[50] also high from your right, deep in behind his blade at his left, so that you strike two Squinting Cuts,[51] one after the other quickly in succession, with a double step to his left. This is a swift technique against slow fighters who send their arms far from themselves.

<*23r*>

The Third Squinter is a Deceit with the Face

In the onset, slash up into the guard of the Day; as soon as you can reach him, at once turn the short edge against him while it is still in the air. Make your face look as if you intended to cut in with the Squinting Cut at his left; but don't do this, instead let the Squinter run past by his left without hitting, and work to his right; or glance towards his right, and strike quickly back in at his left; take your body well out of the way with it. This is a fine and nimble work that does not really admit of writing but must be shown with the living body. **23r.1** **1.54r.3**

Note a Nimble Technique with the Squinter

When you are just about in range of him, execute a Winging upwards before him, so that you come with **23r.2** **1.54r.4**

50 *to his head*] not in 1570.
51 *at his left ... Cuts*] not in 1570.

crossed hands into the Unicorn; as you execute this Winging upwards, lift your left foot somewhat, following the impetus of the cut, so that you come with crossed hands up through the Unicorn; thus you stand as if you intended to shoot through. As soon as he extends his sword, cut from above with crossed hands and the short edge down against his right, onto the foible of his blade; and before it connects, turn your short edge around, and strike with the Squinting Cut, that is with the short edge, from your right, not with crossed hands, at his left side, such as to the arm or face, with a forward step on your right foot towards his left.[52] When it hits, let your blade run out from his left somewhat to the side, and at the same time push your pommel through under your right arm; thus cross your hands, so that your half edge snaps back around against his left over his head or arm; wrench <*23v*> his sword thus with crossed hands from your right towards your left, or cross over his arms. If he opposes so that you cannot wrench or cross over, then let your pommel run through underneath, and catch over his right arm; use wrestling against him.

Concerning Changing Through

Changing through is useful against those who fight with the Squinter or Crooked Cuts. Take note of this: if he does not extend his hands far from him in his cuts, but holds them close to himself in combat, you may confidently change through at a distance against him.

---

52 1570 references Image G.

Item, if he fights with winding, reversing, Crooked Cuts, Squinting Cuts, or any other techniques with which he shortens his sword, or cannot fight long from himself, as happens with those techniques, then before he brings his technique halfway through, you shall also change through against him, to the other side which he opens with this shortening. Thus you force him to parry and relinquish the Before to you.

Item, even if an opponent fights broadly and long from himself with the long edge, but more at your sword than your body, you shall also change through against him to the nearest opening, and let him fall right down with his cuts.

Therefore, whatever technique you are executing, whether with the short or long edge, see that you cut chiefly at his opening, that is at his body. And although it cannot always happen that you can cut at his body, yet as soon as he changes through, you shall fall in after his sword at his opening. Also note this precept in all cutting: when you connect or catch his blade with your forte in the bind, as soon as it clashes, you shall cut in at his body or his nearest opening with your foible, that is with your forward part, to the body or

<24r: Image 8; 24v>

the nearest opening, so that your sword hits his blade and body at the same time.[53] Or as soon as your forte connects with his sword, then as they clash together,

53 1570 slightly different.

you shall turn the foible to the nearest opening with flicking, snapping, and winding.

Furthermore also observe this instruction, when you want to execute these techniques against someone who knows how to change through against you, for example when you send your sword into the air for a Squinting Cut or Crooked Cut, or for crossing, failing, and such like: as soon as you realise that he intends to change through, then fall from this work into the Long Slice,[54] to the opening he gives you by changing through. For whenever he changes through, he opens himself. And when you chase[55] to his opening, then watch for his sword with the long edge; if it comes too near you, turn against him with the forte, and remain on his opening with the short edge. As soon as you have connected, then do not tarry longer, but let it quickly fly away from one opening to another.

> The Thwart you shall also consider valuable,
> with it your skill in the sword becomes complete. [*1570 ll. 63–4*]

The Thwart is one of the chief master techniques with the sword; for you shall know, if the Thwart did not exist in modern combat, then fully half of it would go out the window, particularly when you are under the opponent's sword, where you can no longer attack with long cuts through the Cross. I have already written enough about the Thwart that, if someone knows how to fight, he could derive sufficient understanding from

---

54 1570 adds *that is into the Longpoint.*

55 *chase*] 1570 *slash through.*

it.[56] Still, I am not writing for great <25*r*> fighters or artists, nor have I intended to write this as a historical monument to combat, presenting the art as worthy of serious attention, but only to write a book of instruction. Therefore I will not only repeat the Thwart here, but also write more extensively about it, for the instruction of those who love this art.

25r.1
1.55r.1

In the onset, take heed if your opponent will lay on against you from the Day, that is from above, then slash up from the right Change towards your opponent's face; when he means to strike or cut, let your blade go by your left side around your head, such that your flat faces upwards, and your thumb is underneath on your shield, or the shield lies on your thumb; step with your right foot well around his left side towards him; along with the step, cut with the half edge from your right side at his left ear, so that your hilt stands up over your head as a parrying, with the thumb underneath, so that should he strike, you will catch his stroke on your forte; and at the same time you hit with the short-edge foible across from below at his left ear, as the second illustration shows.[57] As soon as the swords connect or clash together, strike the long Thwart diagonally opposite it deep at his right ear, such that your thumb remains underneath.

56 Meyer is apparently referring to the instances of the Thwart found passim in the work up to this point.
57 See Image 10 (the second illustration after this page)? The Thwart here is delivered from the wrong side, but might illustrate the second Thwart in the sequence. Alternatively, see 14r, the second illustration to the longsword techniques.

Next, note when you cut in or bind at the same time as him with a Thwart Blow, at once seek the openings above and below on the same side with reversing and snapping around again, or delivering a Thwart, crossing over, chasing.[58] For as soon as someone cuts at you from above, you should parry him with the Thwart; when the swords clash together, then reverse, cross over, seek[59] the opening, and execute whatever work is discussed above. Concerning this, <*25v*> Liechtenauer speaks truly in his enigmatic verses:

The Thwart takes
  whatever comes from above.
Thwart with the forte,
  note your work with it.[60]

That is, parry all Day Strokes with the Thwart, or as I have presented it here in my verses:

For everything that comes from the Day,
  the Thwart may parry it.
In the onset, execute the Thwart with strength,
  note also to reverse and fail with it. [*1570 ll. 65–8*]

25v.1
1.55v.1

If an opponent cuts at you from the Day, then deliver a Thwart against his stroke with strength; thus you force him to fall that much further downwards with his cut. When it clashes, push your pommel through under your right arm; and reverse, press downwards,

58 1570 adds *slicing, pressing hands, or wrenching.*
59 The printed version reads *ubersich* (upwards) rather than *uber, such* (over, seek), confusing the meaning.
60 Liechtenauer 'Merkverse', ll. 90–1; Tobler, *Saint George*, p. 89.

and let the blade snap around again, with the short edge in his face, yet such that in reversing and snapping around you remain with the slice on his arms. This technique proceeds well when you do it nimbly. However, if he escapes you upwards too quickly with his arms, then let your blade go around your head, so that your long edge comes across in front on his arms with a Low Cut, as the following illustration shows;[61] but do not release your left hand from the hilt, rather push him from you with crossed hands.

To the Plow and the Ox be quick,[62]
threaten the cut at once against the target. [*1570 ll. 69–70*]

This verse is essentially very clear, like the others, namely that you shall quickly deliver the Thwart Cut to the Ox and Plow, that is to the lower and upper openings, to the left and right, horizontally and diagonally opposite to all four parts, as with other cuts, as I will teach further and more fully in the section on the four openings.[63]

<26r>

Second, this verse teaches how you shall deceive with the Thwart, whether it be from above or otherwise, as follows:

61 See Image 9. 1570 here references Image I.
62 Cf. Liechtenauer ('Merktext', ll. 94–5), the Ringeck Fechtbuch, fol. 28v, and the Starhemberg Fechtbuch, fol. 21r (Tobler, *Saint George*, pp. 118–19).
63 See below, fols. 31v–36v.

26r.1 In the approach, signal your intent with body language and cut a powerful Thwart Cut to his left; if he slips with his sword against your Thwart, be it from above or below, then do not let it hit, but pull back away and deliver a Thwart deep to his right opposite; thus you can threaten the Thwart to his lower left, and hit to the upper right. Item, threaten to the lower right and to hit the lower left with a deep Thwart; thus you can also pull twice, as when you threaten to his left with the Thwart and at once to the right, but hit with the Thwart to the left where you first threatened. In this way you can pull, threaten, and hit with the Thwarts to both sides crosswise and diagonally, according to opportunity and will. And generally you can attack with no cut as surely as from the Thwart.

Note, when the Thwart is executed with a spring,
and you execute failing with it, it connects at your will.
[*1570 ll. 71–2*]

26r.2
1.56v.1 Note, in the onset when you wish to deliver a Thwart to the upper left opening, then spring well up with it, and also let your [pommel][64] go well upwards; thus the Thwart goes deep at his head, particularly when you can use the right body language and spring in suddenly with the Thwart, so that he does not take note of the spring until it has happened, and the Thwart has hit. But if he perceives it and wards it off or parries it, then you will have him diagonally below for sure.[65]

64 Thus 1570; Lund *head* (*kopf* for *knopf*).
65 *you will have him … sure*] 1570 *step rapidly with your left foot*

Item, when you thus strike at your opponent high[66] with a spring using the Thwart,[67] but do not let it hit, running beside his left without hitting, and you strike rapidly with the Thwart at another opening, then you will hit at your will. For before he thinks to parry the Thwart, you have hit elsewhere.[68]

26r.3
1.56v.2

<26*v*>

You shall do the Failer double,
likewise double the step and slice. [*1570 ll. 73–4*]

The Failer is a good technique against combatants who are eager to parry – for example, when you cut at an opening, and note that he slips after the cut to parry, then let the cut run past without hitting, and strike at another opening. Double failing is an artful technique, and a well-trained combatant heeds it. And I will here present and describe for you some techniques, from which you can well learn all kinds of Failers.

Item, in the onset, position yourself in the Wrath Guard on the right; as soon as he brings his sword in the air, cut from your right around your head with the long edge and extended arms[69] at his right side without hitting, and threaten the Thwart at his left.

26v.1
1.57r.1

---

towards his right side, and deliver a Thwart from your left at his lower right opening with lowered body. This you will surely have, if he has parried your first Thwart.

66 1570 adds *and deep.*

67 1570 adds *or else a flat.*

68 1570 adds *provided you do it with the whole body, i.e. use the correct body language for such a technique.*

69 1570 adds *through.*

Do not let it connect, instead go back around your head, and cut with the long edge so that the flat swings well in at his right ear. Now reverse, snap around, let it flit.[70]

26v.2
1.57r.2

Item, in the onset deliver a long High Cut at his upper left opening; when you have almost connected with his blade above in the air with the cut, then transform the High Cut into a Thwart, and strike with the Thwart from below at his left ear or arm. This works on both sides.[71]

A Failer with a False Step

26v.3
1.57r.3

Item, in the onset deliver a lofty High Cut, and when your blade almost connects with his blade, at once transform the High Cut into a Thwart, and along with the Thwart step through out to the side with your right foot, between you and him towards his right side.[72] At once let it snap around again, and strike him with the short edge at his right ear so that your hands are crosswise in the stroke, or cut after with the long edge; and with this stroke spring well out sideways to his right.

<27r: Image 9; 27v>

---

70 1570 adds *and whatever kind of work may present itself.*
71 *This works on both sides*] not in 1570. 1570 adds *These are true combat techniques, from which many fine techniques are executed.*
72 1570 adds *using the Thwart to cut with your point between his arms at his mouth, as you can see in the small upper figures in the following image* [K].

Twofold or Double Failing

27v.1
1.57r.4

Item, in the onset, before you actually come within range of him, cut through beside your right, so that your weapon shoots over into the Plunge; step forwards to him with your right foot; let your sword go around your head, and gather in the air for a high stroke from the Day; cross your hands in the air, and threaten to strike him with the short edge. If he slips after it and means to parry, then turn your hands back around, and turn your crooked edge[73] to a Thwart. Do not let the Thwart connect either, but run past without hitting, and secondly strike his right side; this is called double failing; it takes place[74] together in a winding.[75] If you want, you can break off in the middle to parry or turn to a slice,[76] if he should crowd you so that you cannot come at him with your technique. But when you have crowded him into parrying you, then the double Failer is very good, and proceeds very swiftly.

Item, it is also called double failing when you let it run off doubly or twice to deceive the opponent.

---

73 Lund, 1570 *verwandle die Krumpschneide*. This would literally mean 'transform the crooked edge'; 'crooked edge' is used for the short edge of the dusack, but not normally for the longsword.

74 *it takes place*] 1570 *These two Failers are executed.*

75 *a winding*] 1570 *the air as you wind around his blade in a single motion.*

76 *turn to a slice*] 1570 *to turn him.*

Another with the Double Failer

27v.2
1.58r.1

In the onset start a high stroke from your right, and in the air, before it connects, turn the short edge against him, as if you intended to deliver the Squinting Cut; but do not let the short edge connect either, rather let it run off quickly without hitting, and swing your foible at his right ear with crossed arms. Let it quickly fly back away, and fall on him with the slice to the nearest opening, or on his sword, and from there at his body or on his arms.

Counter against the Thwart

27v.3
1.58r.2

Note, when you bind with someone from above, or cut in at the same time as him, then see whether he will strike around with the Thwart; when he strikes around, then come <*28r*> first with the Thwart under his blade onto his neck.[77]

28r.1
1.58r.3

Item, if he delivers the Thwart from below, so that you cannot come underneath it, then catch his Thwart on your shield by sliding, so that your blade hangs over his.[78]

---

77 Cf. 1570 Image L. Compare the versions in the Ringeck Fechtbuch, fol. 28v and the Starhemberg Fechtbuch, fol. 19v (Tobler, *Saint George*, p. 117).

78 *so that your … his*] 1570 *and push your pommel well away from you over your right arm, and turn your long edge from outside over his blade up from below at his head, as shown by the large figure on the right in Image N.*

On Stepping
Much depends on stepping, therefore see that you give every stroke its step. For when you cut at his opening and do not step with the foot from the side from which you have cut, then the cut is useless. But when you are not really cutting but only threatening to do it, then you should also not really step, but only act as if you were stepping. However, practice will teach you this better.

Do a double step thus: when you have stepped with your right foot to his left, and your technique requires that you should step yet further around, then step quickly with your left foot after the right one, outwards or past behind your right foot; then when you have barely set the left down, you can step forth with the right.

Doubling the Slice
Observe this following technique:

> If an opponent cuts at you from his right, then cut also from your right against his stroke, but with the short edge and crossed hands. As soon as the swords connect, step quickly with a double step with your right foot further around his left towards him, and fall away from his sword with the long edge onto his arm; now cross over. If he goes up and will not permit the slice, then pursue him with the Low Slice on his arm;

28r.2
1.59r.1

<28v: Image 10; 29r>

push him away from you as the nearby illustration shows.[79] This is a true Ancient Slice, and a master heeds it.

Item, when you have sliced an opponent's arms,[80] then you may draw the slice through his mouth.
<*Blank space on page here*>

<*29v*>

From the sword to the body, reverse with it,
twice, or slice on the weapon. [*1570 ll. 75–6*]

This is the true gloss for the previous verse, which tells you to wind twice or slice on the weapon. Understand it thus:

29v.1
1.59r.2 When you slice from the sword onto his arms, you shall at once reverse. If he escapes you upwards, you shall pull or wind your pommel back out from under your arm; thus your sword turns back.

29v.2
1.59r.3 To slice on the weapon is this: when the double reversing has failed you, then you shall chase twice, remaining with the slice on his arms. If he wards this off, then fall on his blade with the slice, and see that you stick to it; do not let him come away without your advantage, but always chase him.

79 *as the nearby illustration shows*] 1570 *with your quillons and shield before he recovers; cut after*. For the illustration, cf. Image 10, but the image is not a close match for the text, and the empty space on this page may indicate a planned illustration that was never executed.
80 1570 adds *from above*.

Chasing is also extremely good,
with slicing, winding protect yourself. [*1570 ll. 77–8*]

Chasing is diverse and manifold, and should be executed with great judiciousness against combatants who fight with long and <*30r*> free cuts, and yet do not observe true art. Do it as follows:

In the onset, when you come within range of him with your left foot forward and your sword in the Day, if he cuts long from above at your head, then do not parry him, but see that you escape him[81] with your head and sword[82] so that he does not hit you. Thus let him miss, and[83] as his sword falls towards the ground with the cut, step quickly to him with your right foot, and[84] cut artfully in high at his head, before he recovers or comes back up. But if he goes up quickly and parries you, then remain hard on his sword, and feel whether he crowds strongly upwards; if so, then let your sword escape lightly upwards; step and strike around with the Thwart to his right. **30r.1** **1.59v.1**

Item, if an opponent binds on you from his right, then take heed when he strikes around, and pursue him with the slice on his arms to his right. **30r.2** **1.59v.2**

<30v: Image 11; 31r>

81 1570 adds *toward the other side.*
82 1570 adds *under his blade while it is still in the air flying in.*
83 1570 adds *as you step through.*
84 *step quickly … and*] not in 1570.

31r.1
1.59v.3

Item, if you stand in the Fool[85] guard, and he falls first on your sword with his own, then remain below on his sword, and lift upwards; feel meanwhile whether he intends to execute a cut or winding against you from the parry; if so, then do not let him come away from your sword, but pursue him, and work instantly to the nearest opening.

Thus note that chasing is when an opponent goes too high upwards, and you chase him below either with cutting, thrusting,[86] or slicing as he goes up; item, if he strays too wide to the side, and you chase his weapon to the opening.[87] Item, in all chasing, if he escapes you, be sure to turn your long edge against his weapon; and take good heed of the slice, for with it you can force him out of all his work.

<*31v*>

Some twice or so
let it flit, begin with it. [*1570 ll. 79–80*]

That is, when you have made contact with him with the slice, you shall see that you do not let him free, but once or twice pursue with the slice, and thus hinder him in his work and techniques. Then when he least expects it, you shall artfully and imperceptibly fly away with the sword to another opening before he realises it. This is a true master technique, which is why you should begin with it.

---

85 *Fool*] not in 1570.
86 *thrusting*] not in 1570.
87 1570 adds *from above.*

Send the hits to all four targets,
learn the pullings, if you will deceive them. [*1570 ll. 81–2*]

You must be well instructed in the four openings, if you wish to fight at all surely. For whatever techniques and cuts you may execute, however good they may be, if you do not know how to break off in each quarter, and to transmute the intended techniques, <*32r*> transforming them into another more appropriate attack, always depending on how he fights against you and counters your techniques, then it can befall that you are planning on one technique for a particular opening, and yet he conducts himself against you such that another opening is more accessible; this opportunity will escape you, if you execute your intended techniques without heeding other opportunities that arise. Therefore always be diligent to fight flying freely to the four openings. For you have three ways to cut and strike, that is with the long edge, short edge, and flat, from which all combat is assembled, directed at the four parts of the opponent; from these arise all other incidental techniques, such as pulling, doubling, running off. Therefore note the following division and cuts, which are struck diagonally and opposite each other.

<*32v*>[88]

In the approach, cut with the long edge to his left ear; as soon as it clashes or touches, pull around your head and cut the second also with the long edge to his

32v.1
Cf. 1. 27v.1

88 The content of 32v–35v is relocated and elaborated in the published version (1.27v–30r).

right lower opening; the third to his left lower opening; the fourth to his right upper opening. These four cuts shall go swiftly one after another, taking the body well with every stroke.

In this manner you should also cut them with the short edge to the opponent's four openings, and likewise with the flat. Note however that you strike with the back of your hand to his left, and to the right with the inside of your hand, be it below or above. You may also reverse or change off the cuts according to your opportunity, for example doing the first to his lower right, the second to the upper left, the third to his upper right, the fourth to his lower left. When you learn to cut these four strokes together in a single motion, you can easily change them off in the first beginning or attack and parry or pull according to your will.

<33r: Image 12; 33v>

Likewise you can deliver the horizontal strokes against each other, be it with the long edge, half edge, or flat.

Now when you have well learnt these four cuts and blows to the four openings, then learn also to pull, threaten, fail, and so on in the following manner:

33v.1 Step and cut to his left upper opening, but don't let it hit, instead when you almost come on his sword with the cut, pull back away in a flight, and strike to his right lower opening.

Item, if you wish to double them, then threaten him above and below diagonally together in a flight, but cut or strike to the upper left opening that you threatened at first. Thus you can pull and fail them to all four targets, crosswise and diagonally according to your will.

Then learn also the Circle Cut, that is a high and low cut together on one side, short and long with the flat as follows:

> In the first attack deliver a long high cut to his left ear; as soon as it clashes, pull both hands up so that your pommel comes through under your right and cut with the long edge from below to his left; step instantly with your left foot behind your [right][89] and bring the haft high over your head.

33v.2 Cf. 1.29v.1

<*34r*>

> Contrarily deliver the first as a low cut to his lower opening with the long edge with a step forwards on your right foot, pull quickly up beside your right and cut the second from above to his left with a back-step on your left foot behind your right, so that you stand protected behind your blade.

34r.1 Cf. 1.29v.2

A Technique

> Item, start a high stroke from your right to his left, but in the air cross your hands and strike with the half edge to his left ear; pull your hands back

34r.2 Cf. 1.29v.3

---

89 *right*] Thus 1570.

upwards, and strike with a Thwart back from below to his left ear.

34r.3
Cf.
1.29v.4

Thus also contrarily cut the Thwart from below to his left with a step forwards, quickly pull up beside your right and hastily push your pommel through under your right arm, and flick thus with crossed hands back from your right above in to his left.

In this manner strike it also with the flat, below and above together on one side; this works on both sides. And note when you strike to the right lower opening, be it flat, long, or short, then your hands come crossed over each other, <*34v*> but for the upper opening you do not come crosswise, but in the Old Squinting Cut, as follows:

34v.1
Cf.
1.30r.1

In the step forwards, shoot through before him and strike with the half edge from your left to his right, not crossed, but overhand with your right hand; pull quickly back upwards beside your left and cross your hands in the air; strike him with crossed hands to his right lower opening from your left. In all this see that you are well behind your blade with your head, with double stepping towards his right.

Thus you can also strike with the flat and long edge from below and above together beside his right, as has been taught, as when you threaten above and flick below; item, threaten in high, flicking or cutting to him above, and if he slips after it, then pull the high cut away and hit in with a low cut on the same side. From this work arise the windings on the sword, namely:

Image 1 (12v, p. 52). Sequence 11r.1, p. 50.

Image 2 (14r, p. 54). A Thwart Cut from the right.

Image 3 (15r, p. 55). Sequence 14v.1.

Image 4 (16v, p. 58). Sequence 16r.4.

Image 5 (18v, p. 61). Sequence 19r.1, p. 62.

Image 6 (20r, p. 64). Sequence 19v.2.

Image 7 (21v, p. 67). Sequence 20v.2, p. 65.

Image 8 (24r, p. 71). A Crooked Cut.

Image 9 (27r, p. 78). Sequence 25v.1, p. 75.

Image 10 (28v, p. 81). Sequence 25r.1, p. 73; see also 28r.2, p. 82.

Image 11 (30v, p. 83). A halfsword technique.

Image 12 (33r, p. 86). A halfsword grapple.

Image 13 (35r, p. 89). A halfsword grapple.

Image 14 (37r, p. 90). A halfsword technique;
cf. Meyer 1570 Image O, 1.61r.1..

Image 15 (39r, p. 94). Gripping over.

Image 16 (48r, p. 101). Sequence 48v.1, the Roarer.

Image 17 (50r, p. 103). Sequence 49v.1 (?).

When you have bound him on his sword, from your right against his left, then remain hard on his blade, push your pommel suddenly

34v.2
Cf.
1.30r.2

<*35r: Image 13; 35v*>

through under your right arm, remain thus further on his sword, and jerk your pommel back out and wind outwards to his head.

Thus you also have three variables, namely outwards and inwards, short edge, [long edge and flat,][90] and on both sides. And you shall know that I have been deliberately sparing in this section.[91]

Also execute slicing off and slinging,
send away the hard dangers with the slice. [*1570 ll. 83–4*]

Now when you thus let your techniques run to all four openings, as I have just taught, then also pay attention to his course, that is to his technique, so that you forestall him <*36r*> and slice off against him; contrarily, hinder and slice off his techniques, until you see your opportunity for other work. The dangers are the strokes from both sides: when you mean to parry or slice them off, then see that you overlook no opportunity; and also do not slice too far from his body, lest he should go through against you.

90 *long edge and flat*] sense supplied from 1570.
91 This remark comes at the end of the section where the manuscript and printed versions diverge; see above, fol. 32v.

Do not rely too much on the Crown,
you will tend to get harm and shame from it. [*1570 ll. 85–6*]

Note, when you parry with horizontal quillons up over your head, that is called the Crown.

36r.1
1.60v.1

When you see that someone will run under your High Cut with the Crown, then do not let your High Cut actually connect, but pull the cut from him, <*36v*> so that he goes up in vain, and deliver a horizontal Middle Cut with the long edge at his arms or the radius-bone of his forearm, if you will harm him.

Therefore if you note that your opponent eagerly goes up high to parry, then act as if you meant to cut high, but don't do this, rather strike quickly around to another opening with the Thwart, flat, or long edge, or behind his arms to his ears, and you will have him surely.

Do the Crown Cut as follows:

36v.1

If someone cuts at you from above, then cut in with the flat together with him to his left ear, so that your long edge slips in on his blade, and your short edge connects; thus your crossbar stands horizontal, and hold your hands up over your head almost as with the Squinting Cut; let it quickly snap back around to the lower opening.[92]

<*37r: Image 14; 37v*>

92 This paragraph not in 1570, and is rather different from the description of the Crown Cut in 1.14r.3.

Pay heed to the slinging; as soon as he makes one side open, then rush up from below at his ears with the flat; slice quickly back down to the opening, or let it shoot around above and go under his blade. **37v.1**

Item, in the attack take heed when you wish to sling in a High Cut or Wrath Cut: should he let you miss, do not overcommit to the slinging, but at once recover.[93]

Slash the Longpoint through powerfully,
hold off all hard danger with it. [*1570 ll. 87–8*]

37v.2 **1.60v.2**

Stand with your left foot forward, and slash through your opponent's face from your right, so that your half edge goes forward, one to four times in succession. As soon as you drive him up, then lay on against him from below, either with a Thwart or the long edge. Note, as you slash up against him this way, take heed if he cuts at you high from your right. If he does this, then in slashing up, turn your long edge against his blade, and catch his cut in the air with your blade,[94] so that it stands somewhat horizontal, your point upwards out towards his left. Step at once with your left foot to his left, and meanwhile push your pommel through under your right arm; strike at his head with the short edge by slipping off behind his blade;[95] at the same time, step up with your right foot around his left, and jerk the pommel quickly

93 *or let it shoot ... recover*] not in 1570. 1570 also has an additional paragraph here.
94 *with your blade*] 1570 *on your forte.*
95 1570 here references Image B, possibly meaning C.

back out, so that you come with your sword into the Thwart or Hanging Point.

<38r>

38r.1 Item, if someone delivers a High Cut at you from his right, catch his stoke with a counterstroke in slashing up from your right, in the air with the long edge; instantly just as it touches, strike around with the Thwart to his left ear. This also works on both sides.

Note, when you thus slash up into Longpoint, then you have the setting off against the four windings which go to all sides: namely if he cuts from above, then slash from below onto his sword, and remain hard in the bind, instantly seek him with winding or flicking. Also note instantly and feel when he means to go away: as soon as he goes away to strike around, pursue him and flick from above over his arm with turned blade, so that in the flicking the long edge stands against his blade; strike quickly around with the flat diagonally opposite to the nearest opening; see that you are at once back on his blade. But if he cuts below, then bar him from above, whether with setting off or sitting on him; whenever it clashes, quickly be mindful of the next opening.

Another Technique

38r.2 Slash powerfully upwards through the opponent's face, step after the stroke to the opponent with your right foot, let your sword shoot around, and set the point at his chest between his arms; protect yourself with the forte over your head; and note instantly or as soon as he has his sword too wide in Longpoint, then attack with the point from outside over his arm.

<*38v*>

Item, slash up before him, and let your sword fly around above beside your left; step and cut from your right from below at his arm. If he parries, wind through below with your haft, and catch over his right arm with your pommel from the outside; release your left hand from the haft and grip your blade to help the right; strike him with the long edge on his head.

38v.1
1.61r.1

You shall let the Blind Cut rebound,
catch[96] the Thwart around, be diligent about the flicking.[97]

Slash the Longpoint in his face; step and pull your sword around your head, and strike with the inside flat from your right at his left[98] through the Middle Line; take your head well out of the way with this, and wind the outside flat quickly back in on his sword also to his left ear.[99]

38v.2
1.61r.2

<*A-hand*>

96 *catch*] 1570 *cast*.
97 These lines appear in 1570 on 1.61r, but not in the full version of Meyer's verses on 1.44v–45v.
98 1570 adds *ear*.
99 *ear*] not in 1570.

Gripping Over

38v.3 Note, when someone binds on you from the right, then press away from you with the slice; if he strikes around with the sword, then grasp with your hand on your shield and catch with your blade over his hands, wrench downwards on your right side, pushing the pommel away from you.

<39r: Image 15; 39v>

A Disarm

39v.1
1.41r.5 Note, if someone binds on the middle of your blade, then release your left hand from the pommel and use it to grasp both blades in the middle, and send the haft or pommel up over his arms; pull towards you; thus he must let go of his sword.

<40r–42v blank>

<43r>

A Thorough Description of Combat with the Dusack, to be Used with All One-Handed Weapons

First there are the guards, which are chiefly four. These are not made so that you should wait in them (as has been partly said above in the section on the sword), but much more as categories to help you distinguish one from the other, namely as follows: when somebody fights from the Steer, he will commonly do or use such cuts and techniques as are designed for the Steer. Therefore when you mean to fight with an opponent, you shall observe from where the opponent fights against you, to help you know with what cuts or techniques you can best attack him to deprive him of the Before. For fighters who deliver their cuts and techniques heedlessly *<43v>* are quickly stopped and must commonly retreat with harm.

And the four guards work like this: the opponent is divided into four parts as has been shown previously in the illustration.[100] The upper two are called the Ox, the lower two are called the Plow. Now when you have your weapon high on the right or left, then you are standing in the Ox or Steer; and whatever you may execute by way of techniques or cuts from the Ox, you can also execute the same from all your other upper postures or guards. And you should not get confused that there are more than four named guards, such as Steer, Watch, Wrath Guard. These names arise from the intent, and should not be taken as being primary, as for

100 See above fol. 7v.

example: I hold my weapon gathered for a stroke up above my head so that the point <*44r*> extends behind me, which I call the Watch - not that it is not in the Ox, but because my intention is thus with a gathered or prepared stroke to take heed and watch where his cuts make him open, so that I may be ready to cut to his opening; thus I may say, he stands in the Ox and holds good Watch.

Item, when someone stands in the Wrath Guard, I may say he positions himself wrathfully in the Ox. And it has already been explained why the names are used, and will be further, but for now I have explained and taught enough.

Next are the cuts, and although I will present or speak of twelve of them, yet there are no more than four chief cuts, from which all the others derive, namely the first is the High Cut, the second the Wrath Cut, the third the Middle Cut, the fourth a Low Cut. For no-one will ever create or deliver any cut so rare or crooked, <*44v*> but he must bring it from above, diagonally, horizontally, or from below. And the many names and variations of the cuts arise from the diverse intentions of the one who delivers them. For example, when I am standing in front of an opponent in evenly matched work and can nowhere come to an opening on him, then I deliver a Knocking Cut strongly from above, not that I want to or can hit, but rather I thus knock to him, to incite him to cut so that he opens up for me, giving me room for the opening. And although it is a High Cut, the cut is called the Knocking Cut, because my intent is only to knock to him to see whether he will open up for me.

Concerning the Four Openings

<45r>
Third, you shall heed the openings and learn to recognise them in the opponent's weapon-arm. Thus you shall note that when the opponent holds his arm too high, he is open below; item, when he falls too deep, he is open above; likewise when he strays too wide to the side. Further, as to the four parts of the combatant, the Before and the After, foible and forte, item the Loop and Circle, slicing and such, this is explained at length previously in the section on the sword: you should also use them here as has already been taught, etc.

Here Follow the Guards, and They Are Namely the Following

Watch [*Wacht*] or the Watchtower [*Luoginslandt*]
Steer [*Stier*]
Wrath [*Zornn*]
Boar [*Eber*]
Change [*Wechsel*]
Side Guard [*Nebenhuot*]

Item, the Slice [*Schnit*] and the Bow [*Bogen*], which are the two parryings, one from below, the other from above.

<*45v*>

The Cuts

High Cut [*Oberhaw*]	Middle Cut [*Mittelhaw*]	Knocking Cut [*Bochhaw*]
Low Cut [*Underhaw*]	Waker [*Wecker*]	Failer Cut [*Felerhaw*]
Wrath Cut [*Zornhaw*]	Roarer [*Brummer*]	Short Cut [*Kurtzhaw*]
Crooked Cut [*Krumphaw*]	Winding Cut [*Windthaw*]	Constrainer Cut [*Zwingerhaw*]

The adjacent illustration shows the routes through the opponent to or through which one cuts. The first line has three parts, namely one on the head and one on each arm, as your opponent sweeps around with the cuts. Thus also the Wrath Cut is delivered chiefly three ways, firstly through the face, secondly through the middle of the opponent, and lastly through the legs, and yet it remains just one cut from the point of view of the one who cuts it, whether it is through the face, or through the middle of the opponent, or through the legs.[101]

In sum, whatever goes from above, whether it is cut to the head or arm or leg, <*46r*> is called a High Cut; whatever is cut from the shoulder diagonally at the opponent, whether it is to the face or body, high or low,

101 Cf. Meyer's 1570 rapier section on these lines, 2.51v–52v, 2.57v–58v, and Image A.

is called a Wrath Cut; and one can deliver the cut with either the crooked or straight edge.

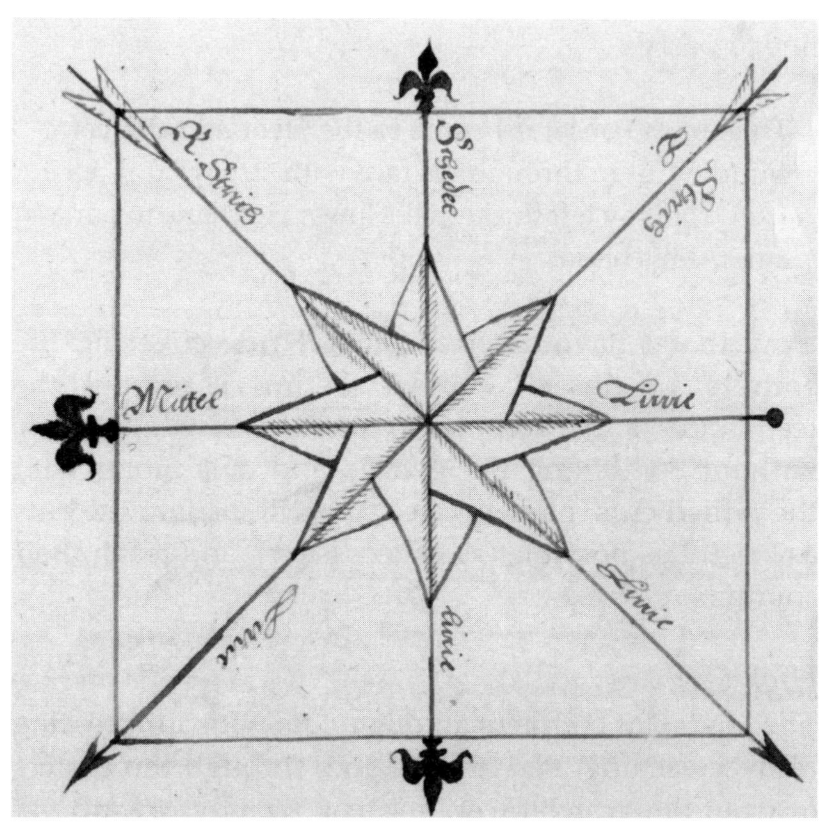

On the cutting diagram above, the lines are labelled as follows, going clockwise from left to right: Mittel Linie (Middle Line), R Steich Linie (Right Stroke Line), Schedel Linie (Scalp Line), L Streich Linie (Left Stroke Line).

For this reason also the names of the cuts are diversified; and also the names are varied for the limbs to which they are cut, as <*46v*> follows hereafter in the section on the rapier; and yet the cut remains fundamentally a Wrath Cut or Middle Cut. And it works this way with all four cuts.

Furthermore note when you deliver one of the four cuts through the appropriate line, whether it is above or middle, then you shall always strike back up the next line to parry.

46v.1 Thus in the onset if I come in the Steer and deliver a Middle Cut in through his face with strength, at once I cut from my left through his lower right line to parry against his hand.

Now that I have given a general rule covering the entirety of dusack combat, before I present the techniques and examples (which cannot take place without combining the guards and cuts along with the pulled cuts, namely deceit), I will explain the cuts as briefly as possible (as is necessary), and teach their counters. <*47r*>

High Cut
The High Cut counters all other cuts with suppressing or overreaching, and always goes through the Watch, or from the Watchtower, and is a straightforward yet artful cut to use.

Wrath Cut
The Wrath Cut is also from above, but with the fundamental distinction that where the other goes straight from above, this one goes diagonally from the shoulder. And this is the true Father Stroke, called the Wrath Cut or also the Battle Cut, because it is the strongest of all.

Middle Cut

The Middle Cut is a horizontal cut as it is commonly named.

Low Cut

<47v>

The Low Cut is a weak cut, but where it is used with speed it is very useful.

Crooked Cut

The Crooked Cut is as follows: reverse your grip so that you hold your dusack crooked; when he cuts or not, step out to the side and cut with the crooked edge, whether it is through the diagonal (Wrath) or horizontal (Middle) line.

Waker

The Waker is as follows: in the Approach, deliver a strong cut onto his parrying, and as soon as it clashes or touches, turn the cut into a thrust in over his parrying; that is called the Waker. **47v.1**

Roarer

<48r: Image 16; 48v>

The Roarer is as follows: again hold the grip crooked as the previous illustration shows;[102] as soon as he goes somewhat upwards, then cut in a pull from below across through his arm aiming at the brawn, so that the dusack snaps back around above as if in a **48v.1** **Cf. 1.10r.2**

102 See Image 16.

wind for the parrying; it is called a Roarer on account of the swift and rushing wind it produces.

Winding Cut

48v.2 The Winding Cut is as follows: cut in outside of his right arm well across over his arm; at once wind back out in a wrenching. You can do the Winding Cut through a High, Middle, or Low Cut.

Knocking Cut

<49r>

The Knocking Cut is sufficiently explained above in the examples.[103]

Constrainer

The Constrainer is a strong taking away from your left to his right, whether it is with the flat or long; I will also present a particular technique hereafter in the Constrainer.[104]

Short Cut

The Short Cut is a throwing in from the left against or over his right; it is also explained hereafter in a particular technique.[105]

---

103 See 44v.

104 See 54v–55r.

105 This appears to refer to content not actually in the manuscript.

Failer Cut

Note, when you come near him, and both of you are high in the parrying, then cut a Circle before his right ear[106] without hitting; as soon as he pulls his shoulders around and means to strike, then cut beside his hilt to his head. <*49v*> **49r.1**

Now follow the techniques from the guards along with the cuts; and I have diligently repeated the cuts even though it seems unnecessary, since I teach about it more widely hereafter. And first follow the Flicking Cuts.

Flicking Cuts

Note, when you stand in the Bow before someone, and he does not wish to cut, then pull up into the Watch as if you intended to cut high; however do not do this, but turn in the air and cut with the long edge up from below to his right arm in a flick, and jerk the dusack back to your left shoulder; from there cut a Weapon Stroke through his right, whether it is to the arm or above the arm through the face; at once deliver Cross or Driving Cuts etc. **49v.1 Cf. 1.13v.1**

Item, however, if he cuts first from above, then parry up towards your left and cut through quickly from your left against his right,

<*50r: Image 17; 50v*>

---

106 *ear*] MS *erck*, perhaps for *ohr*. Cf. 55v.2 and Meyer 1570: 1.33r.2. Alternatively, perhaps for *Ecke* 'corner', referring to one of the four quarters in the target diagram.

whether it be below or above the dusack, thus coming with your dusack by your right side; from there cut back across up from below with the long edge strongly through his arm; or when he cuts against your stroke, let your dusack come onto your left shoulder; from there cut straight in from above.

High Cut from the Steer

50v.1 Item, in the approach when you can reach the opponent in the Bow, deliver a long cut through his parrying to his face, and slice quickly upwards from outside against his weapon to parry; at once work in and out to the opening.

Item, in every cut there are three things to think about, namely inciting, taking, and cutting after or hitting.

Example

<51r: Image 18; 51v>

51v.1 If someone stands before you in the Bow, you should not cut heedlessly at him in his advantage, for he can rush right over you since he is still unweakened. Therefore do to him as follows: when someone stands before you in the Bow, cut the first in through his Bow, not that you mean to hit him, but to incite him to go up and try to strike; as soon as he strikes, you can negate or suppress his stroke with a High Cut; as soon as you have first incited and then taken him, then cut the third long after.

Item, incite him with a cut, and parry his incited cut with the Bow up from below; third, slice after to his opening. **51v.2**

Now if he cuts without incitement, then take his cut with a Suppressing Cut and cut after to the nearest opening. <*52r*> **51v.3**

Item, take heed when he goes up to strike, and cut after beside his hilt to his face; and that must take place while he has his dusack in the air for the stroke. **52r.1**

Item, incite him to a Buffle Blow; as soon as he does it, parry and cut through after to his forward thigh, and come quickly back into the parrying. **52r.2**

Item, in the approach deliver a long High Cut to his head near his hilt, and let it run off quickly beside his right, and cut in long after to his face; and the two cuts shall go quickly. **52r.3**

A Good Technique from the Steer as Follows <52v>

If someone meets you in the Slice as this illustration shows,[107] then step and cut through crooked from your right under his right arm so that you hit his wrist with the crooked point; take the second strongly away with the flat over his right arm from your left, so that your weapon flies back around over your head for a thrust over his right arm to his face; if he wards this off, then cut to his face. **52v.1**

107 See Image 19.

52v.2 Item, in the Approach, cut at him with your long edge strongly through his face, so that your dusack shoots back over your head across to parry from your right; instantly step quickly with your left around his right and cut crooked over his right arm to his head; if he wards this off,

<53r: Image 19; 53v>

then cut forth to his face, or cut over crooked to the left at his head.

Middle Cut with Casting In

53v.1 Item, if someone meets you in the Slice or Straight Parrying as this illustration opposite shows,[108] then position yourself in the Middle Guard on your left and cast your crooked edge from outside over his right arm, and pull the long edge upwards out towards your left through his face; if he wards this off and goes upwards, then cut forth long to his face.

53v.2 Item, note: when someone meets you in the Straight Parrying or in the Slice, then come in the onset in the Side Guard on your left side; cast your half edge over his right arm to his face, pull the second up from below with the long edge through

<54r: Image 20; 54v>

his face, the third a Middle Cut after from your right; if he wards off the casting, then cut quickly to his face.

108 See Image 20.

Now if someone cuts at you when you thus stand in the Side Guard, take the stroke away from your left with the flat; instantly step with your left foot on his right side and thrust over his right arm to his face; cut quickly after through his face or to the nearest opening. **54v.1**

Constrainer

The first is a taking out from your left and a turning away with the flat. The second is a strong cut from your left through his face with the long edge with a double stroke through the Cross. <*55r*>

A Good Technique from the Constrainer

Note, in the onset come into the Slice; do not let him too near you; as soon as he cuts to you, pull through under his stroke on your left side to slip out from his stroke; cut quickly from your left over his right arm with two High Strokes to his head; thus you constrain him. **55r.1**

Rose Cut

Item, in the onset cut from above to go through below outside his right arm, so that your dusack comes back around in a circle over your head; let it quickly run off downwards beside your left; cut from your right to his face. <*55v*> **55r.2**

Item, thrust from outside over his right arm, going through underneath so that your dusack comes back outside over his arm; grasp with your left hand over **55v.1** your right arm onto your blade near the hilt; pull to you on your right side, thus taking away his dusack.

Failer Cut

55v.2 Note, when you come near him and both of you are high in the parrying, then cut before his right ear[109] without hitting in a circle; as soon as he gathers his shoulders and means to strike, then cut beside his hilt to his head.

55v.3 Item, when someone cuts at you, evade with your parrying and let him cut and miss; step and cut through at once outside <*56r*> his right arm without hitting, the second through his face; be quickly back in the parrying.

A Technique against a Left-Hander

56r.1 Cut through outside his left arm without hitting so that your dusack comes onto your left side; instantly, as soon as he cuts, cut forth at the same time as him in at his face; step with your left well to his right.

56r.2 Item, cut through without hitting outside under his arm as before; next take away with the flat from your left through his right so that your dusack flies around above; step and cut instantly with two Winding Cuts together from your left to his right at his face. <*56v*>

109 *ear*] MS *erck*, perhaps for *Ohr*. Cf. above, 49r.1.

Wrath Cut

Note, when you find an opponent in the left Wrath Cut as this illustration shows,[110] then come in the Steer and thrust to his face with parrying; he must ward this off, so cut quickly through his face, the second a high stroke to his head. **56v.1**

A Good Attack from the Steer

Note, when you come into the Steer in the onset against the left Wrath or some other guard, then cut the first in from your right from below crooked through his left side with a step forward; the second also from your right from above, so that your dusack shoots around before your **56v.2**

<57r: Image 21; 57v>

left above your head to the Plunge, instantly cut strongly with your long edge from your left from below through the Scalp Line and a Middle Cut after, or step to him with parrying.

A Good Technique from the Steer

If someone encounters you in the Slice, then step and cut through from your right crooked under his right arm so that you hit his wrist with the crooked point; take the second away strongly with the flat over his right arm from your left, so that your weapon flies back around over your head for a thrust over his right **57v.1**

110 See Image 21.

arm to his face; if he wards this off, then cut to his face. <*58r*>

Low Cut

58r.1 Item, when you have popped a stroke or two with someone, then catch his stroke in the air on the Bow, instantly wrench with the short edge beside your right up from below through his parrying, at once crosswise through his face.

A Technique

58r.2 Note, when someone cuts crooked above to your head, then set him off with the Slice from your right, grasp instantly with your left hand over his right onto his right hand by the wrist, send your hilt up from below and break upwards.

Plunging on the Head

58r.3 Or when you thus have seized your opponent's hand as above, lift upwards <*58v*> and go through under his right, bend towards the ground and grasp with your right hand along with your dusack behind around his leg; as you come to grasp it in haste, lift upwards, so that he falls on his head.

58v.1 Item, note: in the onset come with your left foot forward, hold your dusack beside your right, reverse your grip so that you have your dusack crooked; instantly step, cut in thus crooked over his Bow, wrench downwards on your left side, step with your right behind his right, strike thus outside over his right arm to his face or to his left with a step out etc.

Item, note: when you stand in the right Wrath Cut, then step and <*59r*> cut the first from below through his left; the second also from below through his right, both held crooked; the third from above through his left; the fourth also from above through his right, so that your dusack shoots back over your head to the Plunge; the fifth a Middle Cut through his left; the sixth a High Cut. **58v.2**

In the onset cut from your left up from below to his right arm; as soon as it clashes, thrust in below to his face; if he wards this off, then grasp his dusack in the middle and take it downwards out of his hand on your left side etc. **59r.1**

Work from Running In

Note, when you come close together, then work on him above <*59v*> over his parrying, firstly with a Crooked Cut over his parrying to the left ear. Item, if he parries that, then deliver a Crooked Cut outside over his right arm to his right ear; if he parries that again, then cut crooked under his right arm to his face. The fourth stroke is a Thwart Blow to his left ear from below with the long edge so that your grip is reversed. In these four strokes you shall always be high with the hilt over your head to parry. **59r.2**

Here Follow Some Good Rules for Fighting from the Bow

59v.1 The first rule: when someone cuts onto your Bow, then step with your left foot behind your right and follow with

<*60r: Image 22; 60v*>

your right to his left and instantly lift your haft upwards, thus letting his stroke glance off on your weapon; pull the weapon through his face, so that your dusack flies over your head; step and cut from your left outside over his right arm. This rule can teach you many handy and deceitful arts.

60v.1 The second rule is as follows: when someone cuts at you from above, go up with the Bow against his stroke, turning his blow away on your left side, so that your dusack comes onto your left shoulder; also turn your body well after your dusack on your left side; instantly step quickly back to him and strike outside over his right arm; pull <*61r*> the hilt quickly back upwards to you and cut through his face.

61r.1 The third rule is as follows: when someone cuts at you, make sure he is not too near to you, so that you feel sure you can slip out from his blow; pull your weapon upwards to you and slip your forward foot to the rear one out from his blow, and so take his stroke without any parrying; as soon as his stroke falls to the ground, follow with a blow along with a step towards him; thus the mighty attacker is hit.

61r.2

The fourth rule: note, whenever someone strikes on the foible of your dusack, go up and cut a Roarer from your right to his arm.

61r.3

Item, if someone cuts onto your forte, then turn the tip upwards against <*61v*> his dusack, thus turning away his foible on your right side, and cut a Roarer from your left from outside to his arm, or do the flickings.

These are four good rules that you should well observe in fighting in the Bow.

Counter to the Bow

61v.1

Firstly note: when someone encounters you in the Bow, position yourself in the Change on your left, with your right foot forward; step and thrust up from below under his parrying to his face or chest; as soon as you find that your point is planted, instantly bring your hilt up before your head and keep your point on his body; he will ward off or strike this, so take heed as soon as he goes up for the stroke, and step to his left <*62r*> and strike in beside his parrying. This technique often works as has been shown previously in the Bow and Change.

62r.1

Item, if you are a strong man, then come into the Change as before, wrench away his forward Bow up from below with the half edge, cut quickly after to his face.

62r.2 Note, when someone means to wrench your Bow upwards as has just been taught, then turn the wrenching away down to your left side with your hilt, instantly cut quickly at the same time as him in to his face with a back-step out from his stroke.

62r.3 Note, when someone thrusts in to your face under your parrying as has been taught above, then turn away the thrust; thus you open your face; as soon as he cuts to the opening, go under his stroke <*62v*> near his hand between your hands and jab your hilt in his face.[111]

Breaking In Over the Bow

62v.1 Note, in the onset come with your left foot forward, hold your dusack beside your right, reverse your grip so that you have your dusack crooked; instantly step and cut crooked in over his Bow, wrench downwards on your left side, step with your right around his right, strike thus outside over his right arm high above to the head, the second crooked under his right arm to his face or to his left with a step out etc.

62v.2 Item, when you thus strike someone outside over his right arm as has been said above, and he goes up high, then step quickly out and cut forth crooked in at his face.

---

111 Some words may be missing in this sentence; it appears to describe a 'halfsword' technique, with the left hand holding the blade of the weapon.

A Nimble Technique
<63r>

63r.1 Item, reverse your grip so that you have your dusack crooked as has been said above, cut with a spring from your right with a high stroke overhand in over his Bow so that your right side comes well onto his left side in the blow; cut in a flick back from below in to his face so that your haft remains high; quickly cut away short.

63r.2 Item, when someone stands in the Bow and lets the point sink downwards, step and cut through under his arm from your right onto the foible of his dusack so that your dusack comes onto the left side; instantly take away with the flat over his arm from your left, and cut long after to the opening near his hand. *<63v>*

The Six Drivings

63v.1 The first driving is as follows: stand with your right foot forward and do the High Cut and the Low Cut together so that your dusack always flies around over your head to the Plunge.

The Second

63v.2 Stand with your right forward as above, drive from your left shoulder over your right leg through the opponent's right Stroke Line, from below and above together with strength through his face.

The Third

63v.3 Stand as before, drive the Middle Cut through the Middle Line from the right and left together.

The Fourth

63v.4 is driving the Cross from above together strongly in upon the opponent. <*64r*>

The Fifth

64r.1 The two Low Cuts together from below with the flat through the Cross.

The Sixth Driving
is the double Change, an excellent cut, particularly for someone who is strong at the broadsword. Do it as follows.

64r.2 Stand with your right foot forward and deliver the first cut from your right from above through the opponent's left Stroke Line, coming into the left Change; slash with the half edge back from below through the same Stroke through which you have come, change in the air, and cut from above from your left through his right Stroke over your right thigh; thus the point comes to the ground beside your right; drive back upwards through the same Stroke through which you have come, then change back in the air and cut back from your right through the opponent's left Stroke etc. Thus drive the cut one <*64v*> to six times in succession, always twice through one Stroke, namely once from above and back from below with the half edge. With this changing one counters all guards and cuts etc.

<65r–67v blank>

<68r. B-hand>

Rapier Combat

In the rapier there are seven guards, namely:

The Side Guard, from which you have five parryings: the first is slicing off, the second suppressing, the third going through, the fourth hanging, the fifth taking out with the long edge. From each of these you have the cuts and thrusts, also the deceiving cuts.

Item, Change has four parryings: first, taking out with the half and long edge, plus slicing off and suppressing. Each of those has cuts and thrusts, and deceiving cuts, such as low thrust, high thrust, cutting outside and inside, and straight cuts.

Also the right Ox, which again has four parryings, namely hanging, suppressing, going through, slicing off; along with cutting outside and inside, and down from above.

Left Ox has three parryings: slicing off, suppressing, and taking out from below with the half edge.

Irongate has six parryings: suppressing, slicing off, going through, setting off, hanging, taking out with the half edge.

Longpoint has three parryings: slicing off, setting off, suppressing.

Plow: from the Plow you can set off, counterthrust, take out, seek the opening, double thrust, single thrust, deceiving thrust. <*68v*>

Side Guard

In the Side Guard position yourself as follows: stand with your right foot forward, hold your weapon with the hilt by your right knee, the point forward towards the ground, as this illustration shows.[112]

[Slicing Off]

When you stand in the Side Guard, and someone cuts or thrusts at you, whether it is from below or above, then catch it with your blade well from you with the long edge on his blade by the forte, and slice off his cut or thrust from you towards his right out to the side; and as you slice off, step out from his stroke with a back-step; thus you come with your rapier into the left Change; instantly step quickly further out to the side around on his right side, and thrust up from below to his face; thus you stand in the Longpoint. If someone thrusts or cuts to you, then slice all the thrusts or cuts away from you downwards. **68v.1**

Item, when you stand in the guard as before, and someone cuts or thrusts at you from his right, then slice his blade away from you towards your left as before, thus coming back into the left Change; as soon as it clashes, lift your hilt upwards and cut **68v.2**

112 See Image 23.

from above with a straight *apica* or Scalp Cut slice-wise through his face, so that in the cut you come with the hilt downwards before the blade; this produces a fine pulled cut through the Irongate; at once strike away from you with two Wrath Cuts from both sides through the Cross with outstretched arm and wide stance.

<69r: Image 23; 69v>

69v.1 Item, slice out his cut or thrust from your right towards your left with the long edge as before, and let your weapon run through past your left side, so that the blade snaps back around by your left side into the left Ox; from there thrust overhand to his face with a step out to the side on your left, so that you stand in the Longpoint; from there slice back into the Side Guard or else the Change.

69v.2 Item, if you stand in the Side Guard as before, then slice his thrust or cut from your right towards your left as before, and turn your weapon beside your left into the Change so that the long edge [faces behind you[113]]. Before he recovers from the slicing off, instantly cut with a Weapon Stroke over the opponent's weapon through his hand or arm, and in the cut spring well on his left side with a back-step; thus you come back into the Side Guard on the right.

69v.3 Item, slice away his thrust or cut as before, and let your blade run through backwards beside your left

113 Text evidently missing here, but the missing content can be deduced from the context.

and snap over; threaten him with an overhand thrust; pull back around your head and cut through outside to his right thigh, thus coming into the Side Guard; from there slice or suppress away from you again. *<70r>*

[Suppressing]

The second parrying is suppressing, which is much like slicing off, almost as in the Irongate.

Going Through

70r.1 Item, when you stand in the Side Guard, and someone thrusts or cuts at you, go through with your blade under his, so that the weapon comes to the left side, and slice out his thrust or stroke from your left towards your right, so that the blade flies back around beside your right for the high thrust.

70r.2 Item, go through as has just been taught, and suppress with the long edge from your left over onto his weapon towards the ground, and thrust up to his face, and set off again.

[Taking Out]

70r.3 Item, if you stand in the Side Guard and he thrusts or cuts at you, then take it out with the flat with outstretched arm, so that your weapon runs past with the point before his face and shoots around into the left Ox; from there cut around your head to his right thigh.

70r.4 Item, take out as before and let it fly as before and thrust to his face. <*70v*>

70v.1 Item, take out as before and let it go around your head and cut to his forward inside thigh, thus coming back into the left Change; if he thrusts or cuts further, then set it off with the long edge, or slice through his weapon from your left through the Cross back in to his face.

[Hanging]

70v.2 Item, when you stand in the Side Guard, and he thrusts, take it out with hanging, and let it go around your head, and cut inside to his body from your right.

70v.3 Item, if you stand in the Side Guard, take it out with hanging, and thrust overhand to his face.

70v.4 Item, take out with hanging and threaten him with an overhand thrust; pull back around and cut outside to his right thigh.

70v.5 Item, if you stand in this guard, suppress his incoming thrust, or cut just onto his weapon; cut or thrust long after.

70v.6 Item, slice away from you with the long edge and cut back in through the Cross, or do the Flying Thrust long after. <*71r*>

71r.1 When your opponent does not wish to work, pull your weapon around your head and cut a Weapon

Stroke through his left, so that your weapon comes back to the right into the Change or Side Guard; as soon as he goes after it, encounter him with the work I have already taught. For with the cut you incite him to strike so that he goes out of his advantage, and you thus have a lead-in to the work I have already taught.

And you should note that from this guard one can do four kinds of Takers or [parries],[114] firstly going through, suppressing, slicing off, hanging;[115] and counterthrusting, attacking with the two Weapon Strokes; and every parrying has three kinds of work, namely thrusting overhand, letting the thrust flit and cutting to the leg, and cutting the Cross back in. <*71v*>

Change

71v.1 Item, take out from your left strongly up from below, and turn your weapon in the air beside your left into the Ox; instantly step with your left foot around his right side and send a thrust from below through the Plow to his right hip.

71v.2 Item, take out his incoming thrust upwards with the half edge from the Change with strength, so that your weapon flies around in the air into the right Ox, and instantly send a thrust from below through the right Plow to his groin or forward thigh.

---

114 *parries*] *versein*, perhaps an error for *versetzen*. The paragraph is not entirely coherent in the original.
115 The list on 68r gives five, adding taking out with the long edge.

71v.3 Note, if you stand in the left Change, take out with the flat so that your weapon shoots around over your head; threaten him with the Heart Thrust; pull and cut from your right through his forward leg, and thrust through the left Ox overhand to his face.

71v.4 Item, take out with the half edge as has been taught, and thrust in from above to his face; at once a Cross after.

71v.5 Item, take out away from you strongly upwards and let it go around your head and cut outside to his right thigh; at once cut back from your right with a suppressing cut through his face and onto his weapon.

<72r: Image 24; 72v>

72v.1 Item, take out strongly upwards with the half edge, and cut through from above inside to his hand, and afterwards thrust overhand to his face.

72v.2 Item, if someone thrusts or cuts at you, slice it away from you with the long edge from your left towards your right; cut or thrust after to whichever side you wish, but well extended from you, whether it is below or above, and quickly set off again.

72v.3 Cf. 2.97r.2 Item, stand in the Change, and if your opponent thrusts or cuts at you, go up and parry with the long edge from below with a spring forward on your left foot well under his blade; instantly grasp with your left reversed hand under your blade onto his hilt or pommel, and jerk downwards on your left side; but if he holds strong, then jab with your pommel on his wrist, thus taking his weapon out of his hand. <*73r*>

Ox

When you stand in the Ox and someone thrusts at your left, spring out from his thrust on his left side, and thrust in at the same time as him; in the thrust turn the long edge up towards his weapon on your left side; as soon as he pulls his weapon back, cut with the short edge through his right from below, and deliver the Heart Thrust at him. **73r.1**

Hanging

Item, if an opponent thrusts at your face or chest, take it out with your half edge or flat from your right from above between you and him on your left side, so that in taking out the point hangs downwards to the ground; instantly let it run overhand and thrust to his face; and take out the cuts between you and him through hanging, and thrust as before. **73r.2**

Item, if an opponent cuts to your lower legs, sink the point towards the ground and bar him with the flat, setting off through the Bastion, and thrust overhand to his face; if an opponent cuts or thrusts to your right side, turn the long edge towards his weapon and suppress his stroke towards the ground; then cut or thrust after. <*73v*> **73r.3**

73v.1 Item, take heed when he thrusts at you from below: as soon as he extends his hand for the thrust, then cut through at his hand, and thrust at his face.

If Your Opponent Does Not Wish to Attack

73v.2 Note, when someone encounters you in the Change on his left and you stand in the Ox, cut from your right from below through his left to the face, so that your weapon runs around to the left Ox; instantly take out downwards with the half edge through towards your right side, so that your weapon runs around into the right Ox, and thrust to his face.

73v.3 Item, step to him with the left and thrust through before him without hitting outside your left thigh, so that your weapon comes into the left Ox; take out with the half edge through towards your right side, so that your rapier comes back into the right Ox, and thrust to his face; cut at once outside to his right thigh.

73v.4 Item, if you stand in the Ox and your opponent thrusts to your right, then step with your left foot out from his stroke on his right

<74r: Image 25; 74v>

and follow with the right, and thrust simultaneously with him to his face; protect yourself further with the Irongate, or lift your hilt upwards and catch with your blade over his, and turn his blade from your right in a wrenching on your left; instantly step to his left and cut through at his face beside your left, and thrust back overhand at his face.

Note, when someone thrusts at you from below, step with your left foot to his right side and set off his thrust from your left towards your right from above between you and him through the Bastion; step and thrust in under his weapon at his groin. **74v.1**

Further, if an opponent thrusts at you below when you stand in the left Ox, step with your left foot well to his right as before, and set off his thrust from your left downwards towards your right; thus you stand in the right Plow; <*75r*> thrust from the right Plow upwards to his face; he must ward this off, so step and thrust with reversed hand under his arm to his hip; pull your hilt back to you, and cut through from your left with a Weapon Stroke at his right shoulder. **74v.2**

[Plow?]

Item, if an opponent thrusts at your face or chest, take out the thrust from below beside your left with the short edge through his right with strength, so that your weapon runs above back around your head, and cut outside to his right thigh; if he bars the cut, then thrust quickly overhand to his face; but if he does not bar, you will come through into the Change; if he thrusts at you further, turn the hilt upwards and take out his thrust with the flat through hanging, and thrust overhand at his face. <*75v*> **75r.1**

75v.1 Note, when someone thrusts high at you, turn your hilt upwards into the left Ox, setting off his thrust upwards; as it clashes, thrust inside at his face; instantly let your point sink towards the ground, and let your blade run through beside your left; thrust overhand at his face, pull your hilt upwards so that your blade runs off beside your right, and cut outside from your left through his right shoulder; thus you stand in the right Change.

75v.2 Item, set off his thrust as has already been taught, remain thus in the bind on his blade, and turn your blade upwards against his; wrench to your left side; instantly lift your hilt upwards and cut from your right inside through his right thigh, thus coming into the left Change; if he thrusts further at you, spring with your left foot well to his right side and thrust from the Change at the same time as him; work further at him with the Irongate.

<76r: Image 26; 76v>

76v.1 Item, parry his thrust as before, lift your hilt upwards into the left Ox, and take out with the half edge from your left through his right, so that your weapon flies above your head into the right Ox; instantly deliver a Middle Cut underneath through his lower leg from your right through his left, so that your weapon shoots into the left Ox; take it with the half edge downwards from the left Ox, so that your weapon shoots through a running off back into the right Ox; quickly let the right Ox run through with taking out beside your left, and thrust through a double taking out overhand; come into the Irongate.

<77r: Image 27; 77v>

Now if he entirely refuses to thrust, and you stand in the right Plow, then step to him with your left foot and thrust through outside the left thigh, so that your weapon comes into the left Ox, step with your right well to his right, and thrust in outside his right arm; pull around your head and cut through his face, thus coming into the left Change; from there take out with the half edge. **77v.1**

Three Running Thrusts from the Left Plow from One Side

Thus: if someone encounters you in the Irongate or also in the left Plow, then thrust the first straight in from the *<78r>* Plow outside his right arm, so that your point runs off on the right beside your left through into the left Ox; thrust quickly through your left Ox inside to the chest; instantly let the point run off again downwards through beside your left, and thrust the third from your left overhand at his face. These three thrusts go together in a single fluid action from one side. **77v.2 Cf. 2.96v.1**

If someone thrusts high at you, turn the jab away upwards towards your right into the Ox, step and thrust in outside over his right arm at his face, and in the thrust bring your left hand up from below. *<78v>* Instantly strike out his blade on your left side, and **78r.1** pull away above at once with the weapon and thrust up from below at his throat; if he pulls, then protect yourself with hanging.

Irongate

78v.1 Suppressing: note, when an opponent thrusts at your left, lift so that as he gathers his thrust, the point extends upwards, and step with your left foot behind your right, and cut strongly in a slicing action from above on the forte of his blade; instantly thrust forth up at his face.

78v.2 Item, if someone thrusts outside at your right arm, step with your left foot to his right side and

<79r: Image 28; 79v>

suppress above on it, step and thrust on his blade upwards at his face; if he wards off the thrust and goes high with his parrying, then thrust in over his armpit; if he also parries this thrust, jerk your hilt upwards and thrust overhand from above in over his parrying, and cut to his right leg.

Slicing Off

79v.2 Item, suppress his incoming stroke or thrust from above as before, but in suppressing let your blade slip out slice-wise on his blade beside you in a single fluid action; thrust or cut back in at him from the same side.

Item, if you stand in the Irongate and your opponent thrusts outside to your right arm, then take out with the half edge downwards on your right <*80r*> side so that your blade runs over beside your right as if to the right Ox; instantly take out the second also through a running off from your right on your left, and immediately thrust quickly overhand along with a step forward. **79v.3**

Item, if someone encounters you in the Irongate, thrust at him from the right Plow inside his blade up from below to his face; instantly lift your hilt upwards and transmute the low thrust into a high thrust; cut to his nearest opening with a step. **80r.1**

A Deceit

Note, if someone binds you with the foible of his blade from your right, then thrust at him up from below inside his face overhand. **80r.2**

Item, if someone thrusts to your right, then suppress from your left towards your right, thus coming into the right Plow; <*80v*> thrust from the Plow upwards to his face; he must ward this off; instantly cut quickly with a Low Cut from your right through his left, and thrust overhand at his face. **80r.3**

Item, if an opponent encounters you in the Irongate and binds you, then thrust on his weapon upwards at his face as you run in; instantly let your weapon run around beside your left, and grasp with your left hand in the middle of your blade and thrust to his belly. **80v.1**

Changing and Transmuting the Thrust

80v.2 If you stand in the Irongate and your opponent also, then thrust in outside over his right arm overhand, and in the thrust lift your hilt well in the air; at once as he slips after the thrust to ward it off, let your point sink downwards overhand and thrust quickly under the arm to his hip; if he wards this off again, then thrust back again over the arm to his face. Thus turn the high thrust into a low thrust; you can also change a cut when you wish. <*81r*>

Thrusting the Ox and the Plow Together

81r.1 Item, if someone encounters you in the Irongate, then thrust at him from the right Plow inside his blade from below up to his face; instantly lift your hilt upwards and transmute the low thrust into a high thrust; cut to the nearest opening with a back-step.

A Deceit

81r.2 Note, if your opponent binds on the foible of your blade from your right, then thrust up from below inside his face, so that the rapier runs around beside your right, as if for a loop; don't do it, but thrust back inside at his body.

81r.3 Take heed when your opponent holds his point up high in the onset, and act as if you meant to bind on him; as soon as your point touches, then step and go under his blade with your left arm, thus turn out the thrust upwards from you to the groin; but if he pulls his blade, then protect yourself with hanging and work to <*81v*> him overhand or with taking out and cutting after.

Thrusting at the Same Time in Chasing

Item, when you both stand in the Irongate, take heed as soon as he goes out his guard for the thrust, and step out from his thrust, and follow quickly with your point to wherever on his body he has gone away from, and thrust in at the same time as him. **81v.1**

Chasing

This is a fine nimble work in the rapier: whenever he holds his weapon somewhat beside his right, as soon as he goes away with the hilt, thrust in quickly to the place from which he goes away. **81v.2**

Aftercut from Below

If you stand in the Irongate and your opponent thrusts at your left, suppress him from above; instantly lift your hilt upwards into the left Ox, and cut quickly with the short edge from below through his face or right; afterwards thrust overhand through a Middle Cut. <*82r*> **81v.3**

Item, if someone cuts to your right, suppress from you on your right, thus coming into the right Plow; thrust from the Plow upwards at his face; he must ward this off; instantly cut quickly with a Low Cut from your right through his left, and thrust overhand at his face. **82r.1**

<*A-hand*>

Brawling in the Rapier

Brawling is a compiled summary and true kernel of both weapons, dusack and rapier, which I have here organised and presented comprehensibly and properly, so that anyone who can simply deliver the four cuts long from themselves can well understand and usefully learn from it, even if he has only learned the simple basics. And firstly in this, you will properly learn the cuts to and through the opponent as the illustrated lines show. Secondly when such cuts are delivered at you, how to encounter, <*82v*> parry, and counter them. Thirdly, when your opponent has used such parrying, how you shall take him. The fourth and last part teaches running in or running under the opponent. Item, concerning unequal weapons (as when he has a partisan and you only have a one-handed sword or rapier), how you shall run under him, along with some secret grapplings, so that you can constrain your opponent and take away his weapon.

The First Brawling Cut

82v.1 Do it as follows: stand with your right foot forward and cut from above and below together with outstretched arm, and always send your long edge forwards through the opponent's left Wrath Line as the illustration shows;[116] and note when you cut from above, pull the cut back around for a strong Low Cut upwards through the same line in a single fluid motion; turn your hand in the air so that the short edge <*83r*> faces behind you and the sharp edge

116 This probably simply refers generically to the Wrath Line on the cutting diagram, rather than to a specific illustration.

towards the opponent. Thus do one to six cuts according to opportunity.

The Second

Item, cut from your right from above as before through the left Wrath Line, powerfully with outstretched arm, so that your weapon comes to the left into the Middle Guard; from there deliver a Middle Cut powerfully from you through his face in order to take him etc. Thus you also shall learn to deliver High and Middle Cuts one to six times in a row. **83r.1**

The Third Brawling Cut

The third cut is the Cross through both Wrath Lines, also delivered powerfully with your arm outstretched from you. For these cuts, you shall always stand with your right foot forward, and always powerfully cut after with a Brawling Cut, that is one high and low with the Middle Cuts. <*83v*> **83r.2**

Item, position yourself in the Longpoint for the parrying; if he cuts against your left at your head, catch his stroke with the long edge and at once pull around your head; cut through at his right arm, and thrust high from your right at his face; but if he cuts to your right, then parry and cut to his face or through his body. **83v.1**

Now if he cuts quickly from both sides through the Cross or thrusts from both sides, then parry long from you, and when he has done one, two, three, or four strokes, then at once cut after him powerfully **83v.2** with the Wheel, always stroke after stroke, then Cross and Brawling Cuts as follows.

83v.3 Note, if someone cuts at you from his right against your left, then cut onto it with a strong High Cut from your right and quickly cut after back from your right through his left, whether low or high, wherever you can hit him; quickly get back up for the parrying. *<84r>*

84r.1 Item, if someone cuts at you with Cross Cuts stroke after stroke, then parry him with outstretched arm, one stroke, four, or five; take heed when he pulls back up for the stroke, and cut in between his head and weapon onto his forte, and suppress him one stroke or two; at once cut after with the Wheel Stroke and Cross Cuts etc.

84r.2 Item, if he cuts from below, from the middle, from above, you can suppress them all, and at once cut after with the Cross or Brawling Cut.

84r.3 If someone parries you and does not want to cut but waits for your cut, then cut his parrying away from your left, whether from below or across; this will incite him to strike; as soon as he strikes after, suppress that stroke also from you with a strong Day Stroke on the forte of his blade; cut the third quickly after to the opening. *<84v>*

Rule

Note, when your opponent will not cut at you, you should also not cut the first stroke at him to hit him, but see how you can provoke him to strike; and when he strikes, then parry that blow whether from above or from below, with suppressing or striking out, and you shall quickly cut after that parrying.

Now if he will not allow himself to be incited to strike with a stroke, then cut a Cross through his parrying, or two Middle Cuts opposite each other, so that you strike out his blade; then he must cut; as soon as he cuts, take his cut away with countercutting, preferably on his forte; as soon as you feel that he has been weakened, then before he recovers, cut quickly to his body, whether low or high.

<85r>

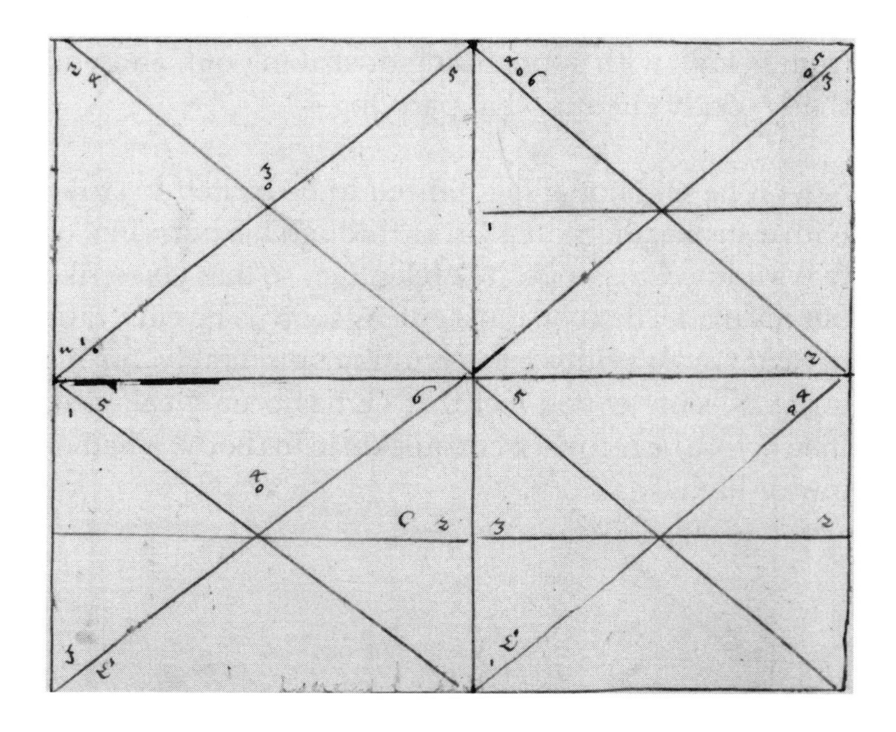

In the diagrams on fols. 85r–87r, the numbers evidently refer to the order of the cuts and thrusts. Cuts are represented by numbers at the origin point of the cut; thrusts are indicated by numbers adjacent to a small circle indicating the target point. An upper-case C (perhaps for Curtz), as in the lower left of the bottom two diagrams above, may indicate that a cut is to be delivered with the short edge. The loops in the lower left diagram and on 86r may indicate a circling action from one quarter to another. The meaning of the 'n'(?) in the upper left diagram above and on 85v is uncertain.

<85v>

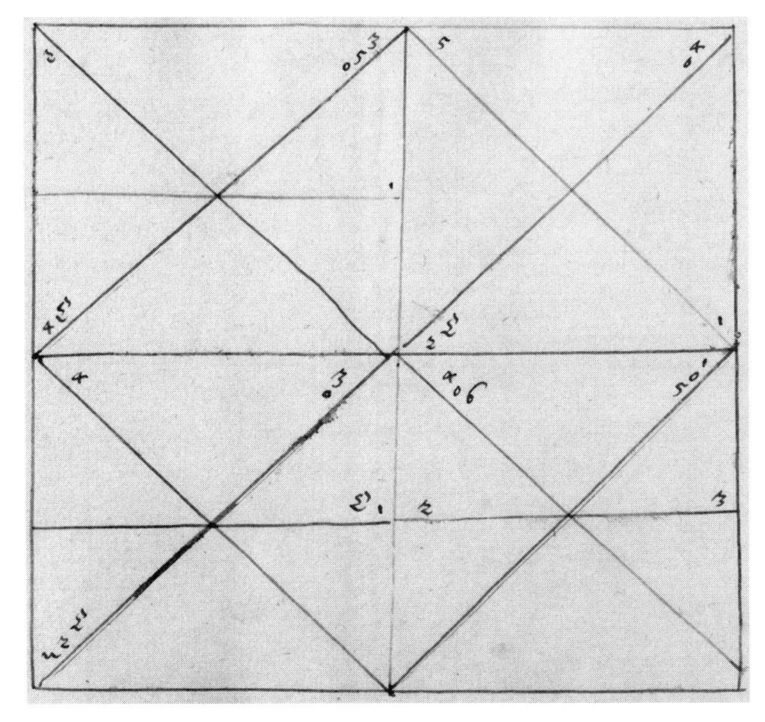

<86r>

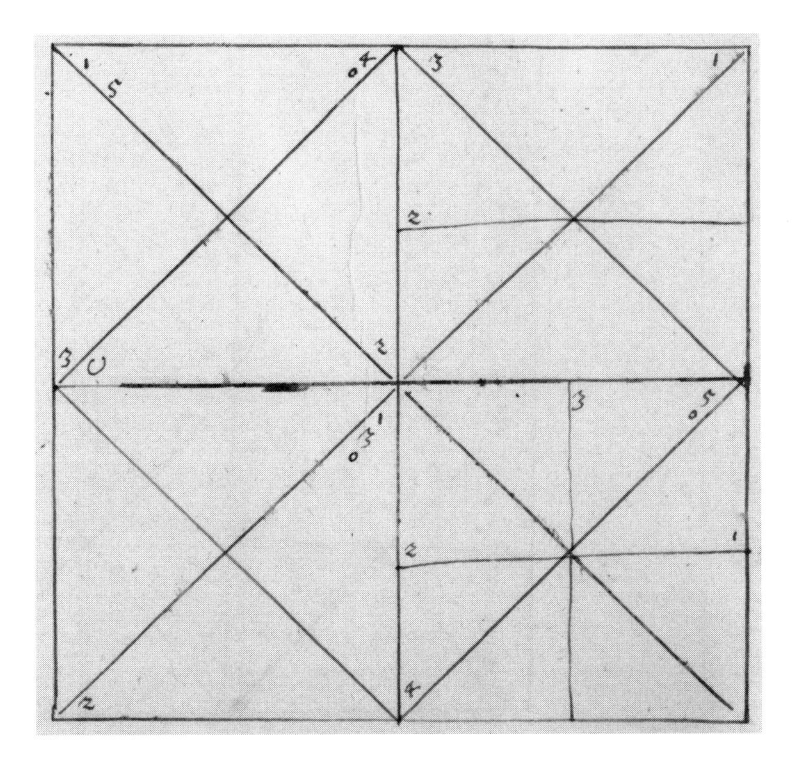

<86v>

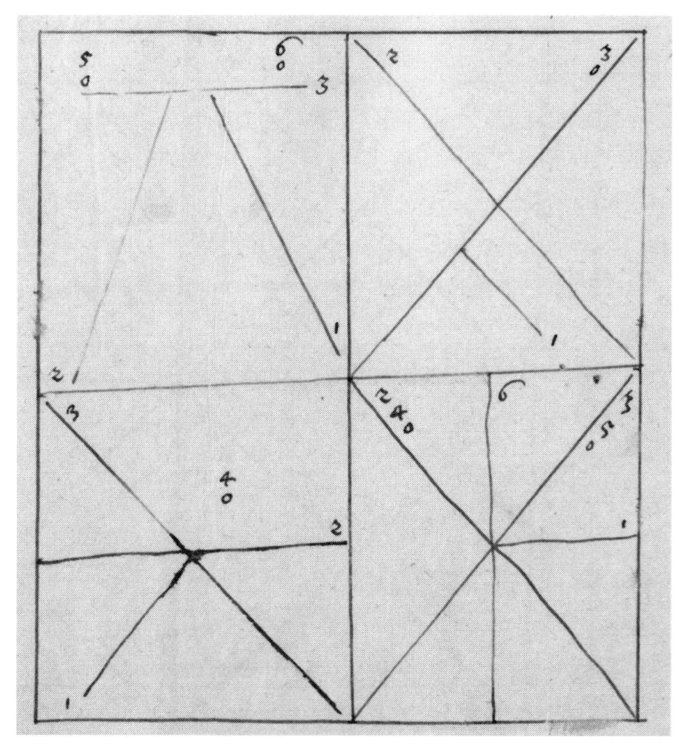

<87r>

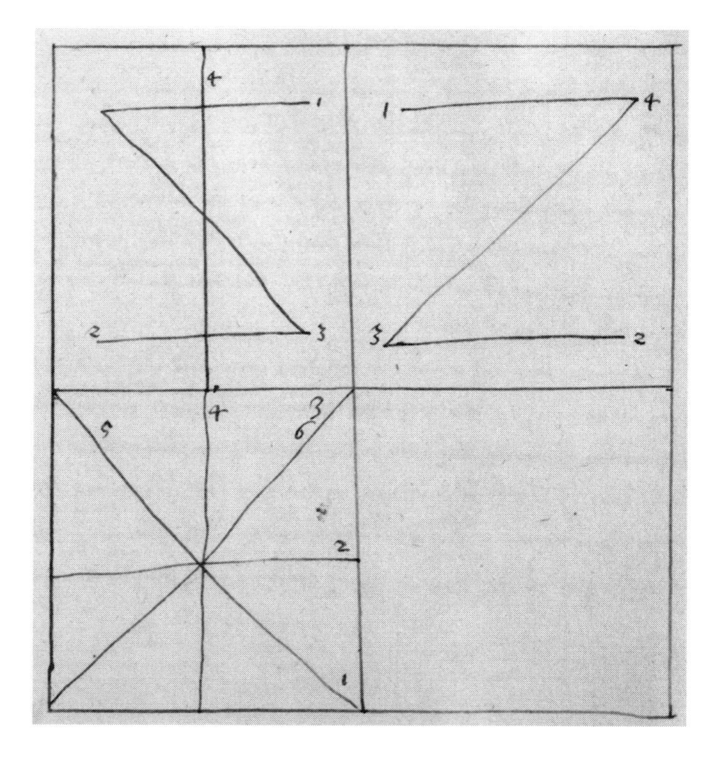

<87v>

A Good Technique

87v.1 Cf. 2.106v.2

Note, if you must defend yourself in an emergency, when someone rushes on you with a partisan and you have only a rapier or some other one-handed weapon, then hold your weapon across before your left foot upon the ground; if he strikes at you with power, go upwards with your weapon and spring under his stroke; and in the spring lower your head out from his stroke, and let his stroke clash off on your weapon, and grasp his staff quickly with your left hand; instantly cut quickly to his hand.

87v.2

Item, if someone thrusts at you and you have your weapon as has just been taught, then go up and set off his thrust upwards over your head; if he pulls out from your parrying and thrusts back, then again turn out his second thrust from above from the Ox on your left side with a great spring forward, and grasp his staff as before.

In this manner you can defend yourself in an emergency against a pike – for in play this thing should not be used, *<88r>* particularly against those who are trained in pulling. But when somebody wrathfully crowds upon you, these techniques are good and work well.

88r.1

Item, you can also hasten to position yourself in the Ox, and from there turn him away through hanging; but note that you shall hasten quickly to him or under his weapon, for the more he has space at a distance from you, the less you will get from him; and if he springs away from you and thrusts at you, then cut away his thrust with a diagonal Wrath Cut; if he strikes, then spring out from the stroke to him.

Concerning the Cape

88r.2 Note, when someone means to rush upon you, then wind your cape around your arm; if he cuts above to your head, catch the stroke on your cape and instantly thrust simultaneously from below to his belly; or if you do not wish to thrust at him, then cut through his lower leg. Now if he cuts from below, fall <*88v*> upon it with your cape and thrust from above to his face; guard yourself with the Cross. Thus you can catch the strokes and thrusts upon all four targets with the cape.

Another

88v.1 Item, if someone cuts or thrusts at you, parry his stroke with your rapier, and, just as it touches, fall with your cape on his blade and hold it off, and meanwhile cut or thrust quickly wherever you can reach him; protect yourself further with the Cross.

88v.2 Item, hold your cape long; if he cuts upon you, wrap the cape around his blade and spring to him with striking etc. If you wish to brawl etc.

Glossary

Only technical senses are covered here; some terms in the glossary are also used in non-technical senses. The German terms are given with their English translations, but variant spellings are not systematically recorded, and spellings are somewhat normalised.

The system I have constructed over the past two decades for rendering *Fechtbuch* vocabulary into English is based on comprehensive study of a very broad range of *Fechtbücher*, and is designed to be compatible with the *Fechtbuch* corpus as a whole. Full documentation of the work behind this system can be found in my working *Fechtkunst* glossary, available online at the following URL: www.wiktenauer.com/wiki/Fechtkunst_Glossary_%28Jeffrey_Forgeng%29.

After	*Nach*: 6r, 10v	A situation in which one's opponent has the initiative. Cf. **Before**, **Instantly**.
after	*nach*: 50v, 51v, 52r	As a preposition or adverb, this can indicate actions executed as a followup to a parry or other technique, or sometimes as a stop-attack that interrupts the opponent's action.
apica		See **Scalp Cut**.
approach	*Zugann*: 6r; *Antritt*: 26r	Refers to the initial stage of an encounter, also called the **onset** or **attack**.
attack	*Angreiffen*: 6r, 8v	See **approach**.

back-stepping, back-step	*Abtritt*: 15v; *abtretten*: 34r; *hindertritten*: 68v	These terms usually refer to a rotating step with the rear foot behind the forefoot (like the modern fencer's *inquartata*).
barring	*sperren*: 7r, 73r, 75r	Refers to an action that interposes the combatant's weapon between the opponent's weapon and its line of attack.
Bastion	*Bastey*: 73r, 74v	A guard with the hilt low and forward, the point angling forward and down, equivalent to the **Fool** in the longsword. Normally used for the dusack, but Meyer here uses it only of the rapier.
Before	*Vor*: 6r, 8v	The situation of having the initiative. Cf. **After**, **Instantly**.
bind, binding	*Band*: 6v; *binden*: 13r; *anbinden*: 6v, 7r	Refers to the engagement of the weapons, typically brought about after one combatant has attacked and the other has parried.
Blind Cut	*Blindthaw*: 7r, 38v	This appears to be a flicking cut delivered from a state of contact with the opponent's weapon.
blocking	*verstillen*: 7r	A version of the **slice** in which the combatant maintains contact with the opponent's arm or weapon.
Boar	*Eber*: 45r	A dusack guard with the hilt beside the body, the point forward; the published *Art of Combat* shows the point angling downward (Dusack Image M), although it angles upward in Leckúchner's guard for the *Messer* (fol. 33v).

Bow	*Bogen*: 45r, 59v–63r	A guard with the weapon-hand forward and inverted, the point angling forward and down; see Image 22 (left figure). Equivalent to **Hanging Point** in the longsword.
brawling, Brawling Cut	*balgen*: 82r–84r; *Balghaw*: 82v, 84r	Refers to a combination of cuts delivered in rapid succession. The term may especially refer to a combination of **Wrath** and **Low Cuts** delivered against each other along the same line (cf. 82v.1, 83r.2).
Buffle Blow	*Buffelschlag*: 52r	A powerful but uncontrolled **High Cut**.
Change	*Wechsel*: 61v–62r, 64r, 68r, 71v	A guard with the hilt beside the belly, the point hanging downward to the side at a right angle to the opponent; see Image 22 (right figure), Image 24.
change, changing	*Wechsel*: 11v, 64r–v; *wechseln*: 64r, 80v; *einwechslen*: 80v	These terms refer to techniques that change from one line of attack to another.
changing off	*abwechslen*: 32v	The action of changing from one technique to another, e.g. changing from one guard to another, or from one attack to another.
changing through	*durchwechslen*: 7r, 23v–24v	The action of moving one's weapon from one side to the other by going underneath the opponent's weapon. Cf. **going through**; **through**.
chasing	*nachreisen*: 7r, 9r, 18r, 29v, 31r, 81v	This typically means an attack into the opponent's preparation, but it can also be used somewhat less precisely for an attack that crowds into an opening that the opponent has created.

Circle, Circle Cut	*Zyrckel*: 13r–v, 16r, 21r; *Zurckelhaw*: 33v	A handwork technique in which the weapon loops around to deliver a second attack from the same side. Some uses of the term may be non-technical; cf. 55r–v.
Clashing Cut	*Glützhaw*: 7r, 19r	A cut similar to the **Thwart**, delivered along a diagonal or horizontal line with the hands high, but using the normal grip, so that from both sides the blade hits with the short edge or flat.
Constrainer Cut, Constrainer	*Zwingerhaw*: 45v; *Zwinger*: 49r, 54v–55r	In the dusack, a **Middle Cut** delivered from the left. In earlier treatises, this cut occupies a position equivalent to the **Squinter Cut** in the longsword.
Crooked Cut, Crooked	*Krumphaw*: 11v–12r, 24v, 45v, 47v; *Krump*: 13v	In the longsword, a cut that angles across the space between the combatants; see Image 8. In the dusack, this term means a cut delivered with the **crooked edge**.
crooked	*krump*: 17r, 17v, 47v	In the longsword, this refers to having the blade angling across the space between the combatants; it can also refer to having the hands crossed. In the dusack, this refers to techniques leading with the **crooked edge** of the weapon, or to holding the weapon reversed in the hand so that the crooked edge is forward.
crooked edge	*krump Schneid*: 27v, 47v	The back or **short edge** of a dusack; 27v uses it of the longsword.
Cross	*Kreutz*: 64r	The pair of crossed **Stroke Lines** used to teach and describe diagonal cuts.

Cross Cut, Cross	*Kreutzhaw*: 84r; *Kreutz*: 63v–64r, 83r, 88v	A pair of **Wrath Cuts** delivered in combination from each side.
Crossed Guard	*Schranckhuot*: 7r	A longsword guard with the hands forward, pointed forward and towards the ground. It is traditionally the final position of a **Crooked Cut**.
crossing over, crossing	*überschrenken*: 16r; *verschrencken*: 24v	In the longsword, crossing one hand over the other to trap the opponent's weapon or arms. Cf. **barring; reversing**.
Crown	*Kron*: 36r	In the longsword, a high parry in which the quillons are horizontal to protect the head.
cutting after	*nachhawen*: 50v	To deliver a countercut after parrying an opponent's attack; to riposte.
cutting away (from)	*hawen sich von*: 17v; *hawen sich weg*: 22r, 63r	To step away from an encounter while delivering a cut to cover one's withdrawal. Cf. **striking away from, withdrawal**.
Day	*die hut des Tags*: 22r; *von Dach*: 7r	A longsword guard in which the hilt is above the head, the blade angling back and upward. An attack 'from the Day' is a **High Cut**.
Day Stroke	*Tachstreich*: 25v, 84r	A synonym for a **High Cut**.
deep	*dieff*: 17v, 22r	In some cases, this may refer to the distance that a technique reaches, but it normally appears to refer to the angulation of the blade well behind the opponent's weapon.
double step	*zwifach Tritt*: 28r	Two steps in the same direction using the same foot, facilitated by a gathering step with the trailing foot after the first step.

doubling	*doplieren*: 7r	To execute a secondary attack following up from an initial one; with the longsword this typically means cutting behind the opponent's blade from the bind.
driving, Driving Cuts	*treiben*: 63v–64r; *Threibhew*: 49v	Refers to a pair of cuts delivered opposite each other along the same line. It can also refer to a pair of **Wrath Cuts** delivered from opposite sides (63v, 64r).
epitome	*Zettel*: 6v, 7r, 8r	A summary of a combat system, usually in verse.
failing, Failer, Failer Cut	*felen* (lit. 'missing'): 27v; *Fehler*: 26v–27v; *verfelen*: 7r, 33v; *Felerhaw*: 49r, 55v	An attack that deliberately avoids making contact with the opponent's body or weapon.
Father Stroke	*Vatterstreich*: 47r	An alternative name for the **Wrath Cut**.
flicking, flick, Flicking Cut	*schnellen*: 15v, 17r, 19r–v, 24v, 34v, 49v; *Schnal*: 16r; *Schnelhaw*: 49v	A flicking attack, delivered with the tip of the weapon using the short edge or flat.
flitting	*verfligen*: 18r	To pull back from an attack prior to weapon contact in order to deliver an attack elsewhere.
Flying Thrust	*fliegende Stich*: 70v	A thrust delivered at maximum range(?).
foible	*Schweche* (lit. 'weak'): 6v	The low-leverage part of a weapon, towards the point. Cf. **forte**.
Fool	Olber: 7r, 31r	A guard in which the weapon is held low in front of the body, with the point forward and angling towards the ground. Cf. **Bastion**.

followup	*Nachfolgen*: 6r ; *Nachdrucken*: 8v	The second stage of an encounter, also called the **middle**.
forte	*Stercke* (lit. 'strong'): 6v	The high-leverage part of the weapon, closest to its wielder. Cf. **foible**. Note that the same word is sometimes used to mean **hard**, which can cause ambiguity.
free	*frey*: 17v, 30r, 32r	In most cases this probably refers to a technique executed with the arms fully extended; in some cases it may mean 'fluid'.
full edge	*gantz Schneidt*: 12r	A synonym for **long edge**.
going through	*durchgehen*: 8r, 68r, 70r	To bring one's weapon from one side of the opponent's weapon to the other by going underneath. Cf. **changing through**; **through**. In the rapier, this is commonly used to describe a parry that involves passing under the opponent's weapon (cf. the modern fencer's 'circular parry').
gripping over	*übergreiffen*: 7r, 38v	A technique with the longsword in which the combatant sends his hand or some of his fingers over his quillon; see Image 15.
guard	*Hut*: 7r; *Leger*: 8v, 10r	A position of readiness for attack or defence; also a standardised position for analysing the disposition of the body and weapon, typically based on waypoints through which they naturally pass in executing common techniques.
half edge	*halbe Schneidt*: 7v, 12r	A synonym for **short edge**.

handwork	*Handtarbeit*: 6r, 7r, 8v	Close work in an encounter, the stage at which the combatants are at binding distance, roughly synonymous with **middle**.
hanging	*verhengen*: 7r, 68r, 70v	To extend the sword with the point hanging down, often in order to intercept the opponent's attack. Cf. **sliding**.
Hanging Point	*Hengetort*: 7r, 37v	A longsword guard with the hilt at head level and forward, the point extending down and forward; probably equivalent to the **Bow** in the dusack.
hard	*hart*: 6v	Refers to when one engages the opponent in the **bind** with strong pressure. Cf. **soft**.
Heart Thrust	*Herzstich*: 71v, 73r	A rapier thrust directed at the opponent's heart.
High Cut	*Oberhaw*: 16r, 19r, 44r, 46r, 47r	A cut directed vertically downwards from above; also called a **Scalp Cut**. Can also refer less precisely to any downward cut, including diagonal ones.
High Stroke	*hoher Streich*: 55r	A synonym for a **High Cut**.
inciting	*reitzen*: 50v	To deliver an attack with the purpose of provoking an attack from the opponent. Cf. **Taker**.
inside	*inwendig*: 32v, 68r	In relation to the body, **outside** refers to the rear of the body, **inside** to the front.
inside flat	*inwendige Fleche*: 19r, 38v	The flat on the palm side of a bladed weapon. Cf. **outside flat**.
Instantly	*indes*: 10r	The abstract term for instantaneous responses intended to gain the initiative in the fight. Cf. **After**, **Before**.

Irongate	*Eysenport*: 7r, 68r, 79v	A guard similar to the **Plow**, but with the weapon held further forward; see Image 28.
Key	*Schlüssel*: 7r	A longsword guard in which the sword is held horizontally at the base of the chest, point forward, **short edge** resting on the forward arm.
Knocking Cut	*Bochhaw*: 44v	A powerful **High Cut**, delivered to provoke a response from the opponent.
line	*Linie*: 46r–v	One of the four lines on the cutting diagram used to teach and conceptualise the lines of attack on the opponent. Cf. **Cross**; **Scalp Line**; **Stroke Line**; **Middle Line**.
long	*lang*: 9r, 21r, 25r	This can have two overlapping meanings: it is used to describe attacks delivered at maximum distance, with full extension, and can also refer to attacks delivered with the **long edge** of the weapon. Cf. **short**.
long edge	*lang Schneid*: 14v	The long edge of a bladed weapon is on the knuckle side of the hand, the **short edge** opposite to it. They are so called because the long edge has a greater attack range than the short. In other traditions, they are often called the true and false edges. Cf. **crooked edge**; **full edge**; **sharp edge**; **short edge**; **straight edge**.
Longpoint	*Langort*: 18r, 68r, 83v	A guard in which the arm(s) and weapon are extended towards the opponent. Also called the **Long Slice**. Cf. **Straight Parrying**.
Long Slice	*lang Schnitt*: 24v	See **Longpoint**.

loop, looping	*Rinde*: 8r, 19r, 81r	An action in which the combatant arcs his sword around its hilt(?). The technique may be comparable to a modern moulinet.
Low Cut	*Underhaw*: 44r, 45v, 47v	A cut delivered diagonally upwards from below.
Low Slice	*under Schnitt*: 28r	In the longsword, a **slice** executed upwards from below.
Master Cuts	*Meisterhew*: 7r	Five cuts in the longsword (**High**, **Wrath**, **Thwart**, **Crooked**, **Squinter**) that were considered especially important in the Liechtenauer tradition.
middle, middle-work	*Mittel*: 8v; *Mittelarbeit*: 6r, 8v	The portion of an encounter after the initial attack has been executed; also called the **followup**, **handwork,** or **War**. Cf. **onset**, **withdrawal**.
Middle Cut	*Mittelhaw*: 17r, 44r, 45v, 46v, 47r, 76v	A cut or blow delivered horizontally.
Middle Guard	*Mittelhut*: 53v	A guard with the weapon horizontal at sternum height, with the point back; see 54r.
Middle Line	*Mittellini*: 46r, 47v, 63v	The horizontal line on the **Cross** (cutting diagram).
on (the opponent's weapon)	*an*: 17v, 80v	An attack made on the opponent's blade executed while maintaining contact with the opponent's weapon.
onset	*Zufechten*: 7v, 8r	The initial stage of combat, in which the combatants adopt their guards, come within striking range, and deliver the initial attack. Also called **approach** or **attack**. Cf. **middle**; **withdrawal**.

opening	*Blöß*: 7v, 44v–45r	One of four target areas on an opponent's body, defined by a vertical line down the middle and a horizontal line at the armpits. Cf. **Ox**, **Plow**.
outside	*auswendig*: 68r	See **inside**.
outside flat	*auswendige Flech*: 19r, 38v	The flat of the blade corresponding to the back of the hand. Cf. **inside flat**.
overhand	*über (dein, die) hand*: 70v	Describes techniques executed with the hand raised and the knuckles upward.
over-reaching	*überlangen*: 47r	To deliver a counterattack that hits by coming in above the opponent's attack.
overrunning	*überlauffen*: 7r, 13v	To attack the opponent aggressively from above.
Ox	*Ochs*: 7r, 7v, 25v, 43v, 68r, 73r–74v	A guard in which the hilt is held just above the head, with the point extended towards the opponent's face; see Image 25. The weapon extends from the combatant's head like the horn of an ox. Equivalent to the **Steer** with the dusack. The term can also refer to the upper **openings** on the opponent. Cf. **Plow**.
parrying	*versetzen*: 8r, 52r	Refers to any action to intercept the opponent's incoming weapon with one's own. Can also refer to any defensive position that closes off the opponent's line of attack.
Plow	*Pflug*: 7r, 7v, 25v, 43v, 68r, 71v, 77v	A guard in which the hilt is held near the belly, the point angling up and forward. The term can also refer to the lower **openings** on the opponent. Cf. **Ox**.
Plunge	*Sturtz*: 22r, 27v, 57v, 63v	A cutting action that finishes by bringing the weapon into the **Ox**.

pressing hands, pressing	*Hendttrucken*: 7r; *drucken*: 6v	A form of **slice** executed against the opponent's wrists.
pulling	*zucken*: 7r, 88r	Withdrawing from the opponent's weapon before or after contact by pulling away with the hilt. Cf. **running off**.
Rebound Cut	*Brellhaw*: 7r	A longsword cut delivered doubly using the rebound.
remaining	*bleiben*: 7v	To remain in contact with the opponent's blade to judge his intent.
reversing, Reverser	*verkeren*: 14v, 72v, 75r; *Verkerer*: 14v	Refers to rotating the hand(s) and/or weapon so that the hand is inverted relative to its relaxed position.
Roarer	*Brummer*: 48v, 61r–v	In the dusack, a **crooked-edge** cut directed at the opponent's arm; see Image 16.
Rose Cut	*Rosenhaw*: 55r	This appears to refer to an action that arcs from one quarter to another around the opponent's weapon. ?Cf. the looping marks on the cutting diagrams on fols. 85r and 86r.
running in	*einlauffen*: 59r, 80v, 82v	To close with an opponent, either to **handwork** distance, or even closer in order to grapple or wrestle.
running off	*ablauffen*: 7r, 21r	To withdraw from or evade the opponent's weapon by rotating the blade around the hilt. Cf. **pulling**.
Scalp Cut, Scalper	*Schedelhaw*: 68v; *Scheideler*: 7r	A vertical cut from above. 68v also gives a Latin rendering, *apica(m)*.
Scalp Line	*Schedel Linie*: 46r, 57v	The vertical **line** on the cutting diagram.

seizing the foible	*Schwech fassen*: 7r	To grasp the opponent's **foible** in order to control his blade, or to control his **foible** with one's **forte**(?).
setting off	*absetzen*: 7r, 38r, 68r	To parry an incoming attack by extending one's own weapon into **Longpoint** and turning the **long edge** against the incoming weapon. Cf. **parrying**; **turning**.
sharp edge	*scharpf Schneidt*: 83r	A synonym for **long edge**.
shield	*Schilt*: 11v, 19v, 25r	The broad part of a fencing longsword blade near the hilt, roughly corresponding to the ricasso.
shooting through	*durchschiessen*: 17v, 23r, 34v	This term appears to refer to a downward thrust executed with the hands upward.
short	*kurtz*: 63r	This can refer either to a cut made with the **short edge**, or to any technique that is executed with limited extension. Cf. **long**.
Short Cut, Short	*Kurtzhaw*: 7r, 50r; *Kurtz*: 17v	A cut that slips under the opponent's sword to attack from the opposite side.
short edge	*kurtze Schneid*: 13r	See **long edge**.
Side Guard	*Nebenhut*: 7r, 45r, 53v, 54v, 68r, 68v–69v	In the longsword, a guard with the grip of the weapon near the belly, the tip extending back and down. In the rapier, a guard with the hilt low, the point angling forward and down; see Image 23.
sitting on	*uffsitzen*: 38r	To lay one's blade on top of the opponent's close to the hilt(?).
slashing	*streichen*: 19r, 22r, 25r, 37v, 64r	To deliver a cut with the **short edge** of the weapon.

Slice	*Schnitt*: 45r, 52v, 53v	In the dusack, this is an alternative name for the **Straight Parrying**; see Image 19 (right figure), Image 20 (left figure). See also **Long Slice**.
slice, slicing	*Schnitt*: 6v; *schneiden*: 28r–30r, 51v, 68v	With the longsword, this appears to mean setting the **long-edge forte** on the opponent's arm or weapon to hinder his action. Cf. **Low Slice**. With the rapier and dusack, slicing typically appears to mean cutting against the opponent or his weapon with a slicing action, with the blade angling back from the hand.
slicing, slicing off (out, away)	*schneiden*: 68v; *abschneiden*: 36r, 68r, 68v, 79v; *ausschneiden*: 70r; *wegschneiden*: 68v	To parry the opponent's attack by cutting against it with a slicing action(?). Perhaps cf. the modern fencer's *froissement*.
sliding	*verschieben*: 7r, 28r	To slip one's sword under the opponent's weapon for a hanging parry. Cf. **hanging**.
slinging	*schlaudern*: 37v	To deliver a flinging cut with the flat tip of a longsword. This attack probably took advantage of the flexibility of the fencing longsword, which could arc around the opponent's defence when attacking with the flat.
snapping	*schnappen*: 24v	To execute a flicking attack with the weapon, probably by rotating it around the hilt. Cf. **flicking**.
snapping around	*umbschnappen*: 7r, 25v	To execute a **snapping** attack as a followup technique from the **bind**.
soft	*weich*: 6v	Refers to when one engages the opponent in the **bind** with minimal pressure. Cf. **hard**.

Speaking-Window	*Sprechfenster*: 7r	Not explicitly described, but comparison to Mair suggests that this longsword guard is a position in which the hands are forward and the point of the sword up in the air, angling a bit to the right; see Mair, *Fechtbuch* (Vienna MS), 1.23r, 68v. In the published *Art of Combat* it appears as *Brechfenster* ('Break-Window').
Squinter Cut, Squinter	*Schilhaw*: 8r; *Schillerhaw, Schylerhaw*: 7r, 11r; *Schiller*: 12r, 20v–24v	A variant of the **High Cut**, executed with the **short edge**. In the final position, the combatant looks sideways at his opponent, hence the name; see Image 7 (left figure). The term can also mean a deception with the eyes, looking in one place while intending to strike elsewhere (20v). The Old Squinting Cut (*der alte Schilhaw*, 20v, 34v) appears to be the version of the cut delivered with uncrossed hands. Fols. 7v–8r, 20v, and 21r describe a variant of the Squinter with crossed arms delivered from the attacker's left side - normally the arms should be uncrossed from this side, leaving some doubt as to how Meyer uses the term.
Steer	*Stier*: 52r–v, 56v	A dusack guard equivalent to **Ox**, with the hilt beside the head and the point towards the opponent; see Image 19, Image 21 (left figures).
straight edge	*gerade Schneid*: 46r	See **long edge**.

Straight Parrying	*gerade Versatzung*: 53v	A guard in which the weapon is held forward, and the point angles somewhat upward. In the dusack, this can also be called the **Slice**.
striking around	*umbschlagen*: 7r, 9r	To **pull** away from the **bind** to attack to another opening.
striking away	*streichen (von sich) wegk*: 68v	To deliver a blow while opening the distance to get out of range of the opponent. Cf. **cutting away**.
Stroke Line, Stroke	*Strichlini*: 46r, 63v, 64r; *Strich*: 64r–v	The diagonal **line** on the cutting diagram. Also called the **Wrath Line**.
suppress-ing, Suppress-ing Cut	*dempffen*: 47r, 68r, 78v, 79v, 80r, 84r; *Dempffhaw*: 51v	Refers to a **High Cut** delivered against an incoming attack as a countercutting parry, perhaps specifically at the opponent's **forte** (cf. 78v, 84r).
Tag, Tag-Hit	*Zeckrur*: 17r	A flicking attack with the weapon. Cf. **flick**.
Taker	*Nemer*: 71r	Meyer's published *Art of Combat* classifies cuts as 'Inciter' (*Reitzer*), 'Taker' (*Nemer*), and 'Hitter' (*Treffer*) typically used in combination (2.16r, 99r); this division is alluded to on fol. 51v. The Inciter provokes the opponent to leave his guard to attack, the Taker intercepts the attack, and the Hitter takes advantage of the opening to hit the opponent. Cf. **taking**.
taking, taking away (out)	*nemen*: 10v, 50v; *wegknemen*: 63r; *ausnemen*: 68r	To intercept the opponent's attack or strike his weapon out to the side. Can also be used more loosely to mean 'negate' (61r, 82v).

through	*durch*: 13v, 17v, 21r	Refers to motion from one side of the opponent's weapon or body to the other, usually executed underneath the opponent's weapon. Cf. **changing through**; **going through**; **winding through**.
Thwart, Thwart Blow	*Zwirch*: 8v, 24v–26r; *Zwerchhaw*: 7r; *Zwirchschlag*: 25r, 59v	A helicoptering cut delivered with the hands high and the thumb underneath the **shield**, with the **short edge** when delivered from the right, with the **long edge** from the left; see 28v.
transmuting	*mutieren*: 80r, 80v, 81r	To change the line of attack, typically between high and low.
turning (away, out)	*wenden*: 74v; *abwenden*: 60v, 61v; *auswenden*: 81r, 88r	To deflect the opponent's weapon.
under (an opponent, an opponent's weapon, etc.)	*under*: 13r, 24v, 72v, 82v, 87v	Refers to a situation in which one is too close to the opponent for him to deliver a fully extended cut.
Unicorn	*Einhorn*: 23r	A longsword guard with the hands high and forward and the point angling upward - the final position of a **Low Cut**.
Waker	*Wecker*: 45v, 47v	In the dusack, a cut that is transformed into a thrust, delivered while maintaining contact with the opponent's blade. This seems to be the normal meaning of the term in the prior dusack sources, although it is worth noting that the cut occupies the same place in the Leckküchner system as the **Crooked** in the longsword.

War	*Krieg*: 18r	The second stage of an encounter, once the **attack** has been executed and the combatants are at **binding** distance. Also called **followup**, **handwork**, or **middle**.
Watch, Watchtower	*Wacht*: 43v–44r, 45r, 47r; *Luoginslandt*: 45r, 47r	A dusack guard with the hilt above the head, the point angling backward. Equivalent to **Day** in the longsword.
Weapon Stroke	*Wehrstreich*: 49v, 71r	Another name for the **Wrath Cut**; the term could also be interpreted as 'Defence Stroke'.
Wheel, Wheel Stroke	*Radt*: 83v; *Radtstreich*: 84r	A rotating action with the weapon, perhaps comparable to the modern moulinet. Cf. *Radt* in Lecküchner, *Fechtbuch*, fol. 66r; *Rad* in Mair, *Fechtbuch* (Vienna MS), vol. 1, fol. 173v; *Redel* in the Ringeck Fechtbuch, fol. 52r. Cf. **loop**.
wind, winding	*winden*: 7r, 24v	From the **bind**, to remain in contact while winding one's blade around the opponent's weapon for a **followup** attack. The same term can be used of a similar manoeuvre that leads with the pommel (cf. **winding through**).
Winding Cut	*Windthaw*: 7r, 48v	A cut executed behind the opponent's blade from the **bind**(?).
winding through	*durchwinden*: 17r	To **wind** the pommel underneath the opponent's blade to the opposite side to catch over the opponent's arm or weapon.

Winging (upwards)	*aufflüglen*: 23r	Some kind of rising cut. Meyer's meaning is unclear, but the term seems to be related to a Wing Cut (*Flügelhauw*, *ictus alaris*) mentioned by other sixteenth-century sources. See the Egenolff Fechtbuch (?c. 1535), fol. 5r; Mair, *Fechtbuch* (Vienna MS), vol. 1, fols. 4v, 18r, 20r, 27v; Wassmannsdorf, *Fechtschulen*, pp. 51, 57.
withdrawal	*Abziehen*: 6r; *Abzug*: 8v	Refers to the third and final stage of an encounter, in which the combatant opens the distance while delivering a cut. Cf. **cutting away**; **middle**; **onset**.
Wrath Cut	*Zornhaw*: 7r, 45v, 46r, 47r, 56v, 58v	A cut delivered diagonally downwards; also called the **Father Stroke**. Sometimes used to mean **Wrath Guard**.
Wrath Guard, Wrath	*Zornhut*: 44r; *Zornleger*: 7r; *Zorn*: 56v	A longsword and dusack guard in which the weapon hangs back over the rear shoulder; see Image 21 (right figure).
Wrath Line	*Zornlini*: 47v	A synonym for **Stroke Line**.
wrenching	*aussreissen*: 7r	To forcibly move the opponent's weapon; see Image 3 (right figure). Note that the German does not carry any particular connotation of circular motion, but may imply the use of the **short edge** and/or a **pulling** motion, since *reissen* can also mean **slashing**. This doubtless reflects the mechanical advantage of pulling with the short edge of a weapon for a forcing technique.
Wrist Cut	*Knuchelhaw*: 7r	A quick attack with the longsword delivered at the opponent's exposed forearms.

German–English Word List

German	*English*
ablauffen	**running off**
absetzen	**setting off**
Abtritt; abtretten	**back-stepping**
abwechslen	**changing off**
abziehen; Abzug	**withdrawal**
an	**on**
anbinden	**binding**
Angreiffen	**attack**
Antritt	**approach**
aufflüglen	**Winging**
aussreissen	**wrenching**
auswendig; auswendige Fleche	**outside, outside flat**
balgen; Balghaw	**brawling, Brawling Cut**
Band; binden	**bind, binding**
Bastey	**Bastion**
bleiben	**remaining**
Blindthaw	**Blind Cut**
Blöß	**opening**
Bochhaw	**Knocking Cut**
Bogen	**Bow**
Brellhaw	**Rebound Cut**
Brummer	**Roarer**
Buffelschlag	**Buffle Blow**
dempffen; Dempffhaw	**suppressing, Suppressing Cut**
dieff	**deep**
doplieren	**doubling**
drucken	**pressing**
durch	**through**
durchgehen	**going through**

German	*English*
durchschiessen	**shooting through**
durchwechslen	**changing through**
durchwinden	**winding through**
Eber	**Boar**
Einhorn	**Unicorn**
einlauffen	**running in**
einwechslen	**changing**
Eysenport	**Irongate**
felen; Fehler; Felerhaw	**failing, Failer, Failer Cut**
fliegende Stich	**Flying Thrust**
frey	**free**
gantz Schneidt	**full edge**
gerade Schneid	**straight edge**
gerade Versatzung	**Straight Parrying**
Glützhaw	**Clashing Cut**
halbe Schneidt	**half edge**
Handtarbeit	**handwork**
hart	**hard**
hawen sich von; hawen sich weg; (ab)hawen	**cutting away**
Hendttrucken	**pressing hands**
Hengetort	**Hanging Point**
Herzstich	**Heart Thrust**
hindertritten	**back-stepping**
hoher Streich	**High Stroke**
Hut	**guard**
indes	**Instantly**
inwendig; inwendige Fleche	**inside, inside flat**
Knuchelhaw	**Wrist Cut**
Kreutz; Kreutzhaw	**Cross, Cross Cut**
Krieg	**War**
Kron	**Crown**
krump	**crooked**
krump Schneid	**crooked edge**

German	*English*
Krumphaw; Krump	**Crooked Cut, Crooked**
kurtz; kurtze Schneid	**short, short edge**
Kurtzhaw; Kurtz	**Short Cut, Short**
lang; lange Schneid; langer Schnitt	**long, long edge, Long Slice**
Langort	**Longpoint**
Leger	**guard**
Linie	**line**
Luoginslandt	**Watchtower**
Meisterhew	**Master Cuts**
Mittel; Mittelarbeit	**middle, middle-work**
Mittelhaw	**Middle Cut**
Mittelhut	**Middle Guard**
Mittellini	**Middle Line**
mutieren	**transmuting**
nach	**after**
Nachfolgen; Nachdrucken	**followup**
nachhawen	**cutting after**
nachreisen	**chasing**
Nebenhut	**Side Guard**
nemen; Nemer; wegnemen	**taking, Taker, taking away**
Oberhaw	**High Cut**
Ochs	**Ox**
Olber	**Fool**
Pflug	**Plow**
Radt; Radtstreich	**Wheel, Wheel Stroke**
reitzen	**inciting**
Rinde	**loop, looping**
Rosenhaw	**Rose Cut**
scharpf Schneidt	**sharp edge**
Schedel Linie	**Scalp Line**
Schedelhaw; Scheideler	**Scalp Cut, Scalper**
Schilhaw; Schillerhaw, Schylerhaw; Schiller	**Squinter Cut, Squinter**

German	***English***
Schilt	**shield**
schlaudern	**slinging**
Schlüssel	**Key**
schnappen	**snapping**
schneiden; abschneiden; ausschneiden; wegschneiden	**slicing, slicing off, slicing out, slicing away**
schnellen; Schnal; Schnelhaw	**flicking, flick, Flicking Cut**
Schnitt; schneiden	**Slice, slicing**
Schranckhuot	**Crossed Guard**
Schwech fassen	**seizing the foible**
Schweche	**foible**
sperren	**barring**
Sprechfenster	**Speaking-Window**
Stercke	**forte**
Stier	**Steer**
streichen	**slashing**
streichen (von sich) wegk	**striking away from**
Strichlini; Strich	**Stroke Line, Stroke**
Sturtz	**Plunge**
Tachstreich	**Day Stroke**
treiben; Threibhew	**driving, Driving Cuts**
über (dein, die) hand	**overhand**
übergreiffen	**gripping over**
überlangen	**overreaching**
überlauffen	**overrunning**
überschrenken	**crossing over**
uffsitzen	**sitting on**
umbschlagen	**striking around**
umbschnappen	**snapping around**
under	**under**
under Schnitt	**Low Slice**
Underhaw	**Low Cut**
Vatterstreich	**Father Stroke**

German	*English*
verfelen	**failing**
verfligen	**flitting**
verhengen	**hanging**
verkeren; Verkerer	**reversing, Reverser**
verscheiben	**sliding**
verschrencken	**crossing**
versetzen	**parrying**
verstillen	**blocking**
von Dach	**Day**
Vor	**Before**
Wacht	**Watch**
Wechsel; wechseln	**Change, changing**
Wecker	**Waker**
Wehrstreich	**Weapon Stroke**
weich	**soft**
wenden; abwenden; auswenden	**turning, turning away, turning out**
winden	**winding**
Windthaw	**Winding Cut**
Zeckrur	**Tag, Tag-Hit**
Zettel	**epitome**
Zornhaw	**Wrath Cut**
Zornhut; Zornleger; Zorn	**Wrath Guard, Wrath**
Zornlini	**Wrath Line**
zucken	**pulling**
Zufechten	**onset**
Zugann	**approach**
Zurckelhaw	**Circle Cut**
zwifach Tritt	**double step**
Zwingerhaw; Zwinger	**Constrainer Cut, Constrainer**
Zwirch; Zwerchhaw; Zwirchschlag	**Thwart, Thwart Blow**
Zyrckel	**Circle**

Appendix A

Meyer's Rapier Treatise in the Rostock Manuscript

The following text appears on folios 123r–127r of Meyer's Rostock Fechtbuch (Rostock Universitätsbibliothek, Mss. var. 82), probably in Meyer's own hand. The text is incomplete; it may represent the initial stages of Meyer's next iteration of his pedagogy for the rapier, after putting the finishing touches on the published *Art of Combat* early the same year. The first section echoes the foreword to the printed book (sig. B1v–B2v). This text, along with the Lund manuscript and published *Art of Combat*, are today the only known surviving combat treatises by Meyer.

Combat with the Rapier, Compiled from Italian, Spanish, Neapolitan, French, and German Sources, Along with its Basis and True Foundation

By Joachim Meyer
1570

Along with some fine techniques from each nation as personally learned and presented by the well-born lord, lord Heinrich Graf von Eberstein and Naugard.

The Entire Contents and Foundation on which Rapier Combat Rests

Combat with all weapons rests chiefly on two techniques. The first technique is the cuts and thrusts, with which you strive to defeat your opponent. The second technique is the parryings, with which you should deflect and parry the aforementioned cuts and thrusts away from you without harm, making space for yourself with this parrying and deflection so that you can safely execute on him the first chief technique, i.e. the cuts and thrusts.

The cuts and thrusts (as covered in the first chief technique) are carried out in four chief ways: i.e. the first from above, the second diagonally downward, the third horizontally, and the fourth from below. Even though these are presented and distinguished with many different names, they all still fall under the four principal cuts and thrusts.

There are also just four types of parryings, namely, the first from above, the second diagonal, the third horizontal, the fourth from below. Each of these parryings is also presented and described with various names based on its individual type.

These two elements lead to the third, namely *mutacio* [changing] and transforming, from which come the techniques that follow, i.e. binding, remaining, going after, going through, and setting off, changing through and around, pulling, winding, chasing, falling in, jerking, and jabbing.

In the practice and praxis of these techniques you should pay good heed to the following rules, according to which you should always diligently guide yourself.

The First Rule
You should conduct all your cuts and thrusts such that you do not lose control of your weapon or overcommit with it.

The Second Rule
You should not cut to the body until you have made yourself secure with parrying, not only to cut or thrust to his body, but so that after delivering the cut you can recover your weapon and body without harm.

The Third Rule
You should also not let him touch or bind your blade, unless you want to intercept, catch, or take his blade. For whenever the blades touch and hit in the bind, you should have a sure opening, otherwise your art is false.

The Fourth Rule
In all combat you should take heed of the opponent's limbs, for whenever he gathers them you have an opportunity for chasing. Also, in chasing you should change around his hilt, and learn to step correctly for everything.

Guarding by the Leg
If you are holding your rapier with the pommel by your leg so that the point goes up towards the opponent, be diligent about the following work: first, do not let him intercept or touch your blade, but always go through; and as you go through, on whatever side he thrusts, go in on the other side, stepping out from his weapon. If he goes after your blade as you go through, then

change through short, and fall on his blade, and thrust to his body. If he falls on your blade as you go through, note first: if he falls on the foible, strike around on his blade; if he falls on the forte, jerk his weapon around on the other side. If he falls on the middle, then let it run through, and fall back on it with suppressing, and work at once to the opening.

Appendix B

Joachim Meyer, free fencer, citizen of Strassburg (?1537–1571)

By Olivier Dupuis [transl. J. L. Forgeng][1]

Abstract

Among all the German authors of fencing manuals in the sixteenth century, Joachim Meyer was until now the subject of a strange paradox: he was without doubt the author on whom we had the least information, even though his fencing book was one of the most - if not the most - studied. This article brings to light unedited biographical information that allows us to better perceive the period when Meyer lived in Strassburg. Having evidently come from Basel in the process of becoming a cutler, he became a citizen when he married a widow in 1560. He pursued his career as a cutler and fencer until 1570, the year when he published the book that made him famous. The execution of this work left him heavily in debt, and the search for potential purchasers

---

1 Original version published as Olivier Dupuis, 'Joachim Meyer, escrimeur libre, bourgeois de Strasbourg (1537?–1571)', in *Maîtres et techniques de combat à la fin du Moyen Âge et au début de la Renaissance*, ed. Fabrice Cognot. Paris: Association pour l'Edition et la Diffusion des Etudes Historiques, 2006, pp. 107–20. This translation is here published with the original author's permission and collaboration, and has been slightly updated relative to the original French version (including some additional transcriptions and translations), and reformatted for this book.

prompted him to leave Strassburg under contract as a fencing master for the court of the Duke of Mecklenburg-Schwerin. Unfortunately, death took him shortly after his arrival, leaving his widow and his brother-in-law to discharge his debts.

Two training longswords and a dusack. Marginalia accompanying the minutes of a discussion of the Council and the Twenty-One on 2 December 1559 concerning a fencing contest.
AS 1R22, fol. 533v.
Reproduced by permission of Les Archives de la ville et de l'Eurométropole de Strasbourg.

In 1570 Joachim Meyer, a citizen of Strassburg, published in that city one of the most important and sumptuous fencing treatises of the sixteenth century, making the transition in this work between the Liechtenauer fencing tradition and the new fencing, of Italian origin, which was distinguished in particular by the appearance of the rapier.[2]

It is difficult to judge the audience of the work, but the number of reprints and references can serve as an indication. Joachim Meyer's work was reprinted in

2 Meyer, *Gründtliche Beschreibung.*

Augsburg in 1600. An echo in the fencing environment is offered by the references to Meyer's treatise in other works: in 1579 that of von Günterode,[3] and in 1632 that of Luis Pacheco de Narváez.[4] Additionally, the fencing treatise of Jacob Sutor in 1612 and that of Theodor Verolinus in 1679 are in large part lesser-quality derivatives of Meyer's *Art of Combat,* confirming the importance that this work had in German, not to say European, fencing.[5]

Nonetheless it appears that Joachim Meyer did not benefit from this success during his lifetime.

Meyer's Biography

Information drawn largely from the municipal archives of Strasbourg[6] affords more precise knowledge of this author's life, particularly for the period between the appearance of his work (after 24 February 1570 - the date mentioned in the introduction to his book) and his death on 24 February 1571, exactly one year later.[7]

The first mention of Joachim Meyer in Strassburg is found in his deed of marriage, which took place in the church of St William of Strassburg on 4 June 1560. His wife, Apollonia Rülmann, was the widow of Jacob

---

3 Günterode, *De veris principiis,* sig. C3r–v; Anglo, *Martial Arts,* p. 92.

4 Pacheco de Narváez, *Nueva ciencia,* sig. §5r, ¶¶3r, pp. 403, 490, 578, 657. See also Marcelli, *Regole della Scherma,* sig. B2r.

5 Anglo, *Martial Arts,* p. 52.

6 Today, Strasbourg is part of France, but in Meyer's day the city was German-speaking and known to its inhabitants as Strassburg.

7 All the dates in this article are the ones given in the sources, at a time when the Julian calendar was in effect. One must add ten days to convert to the modern Gregorian calendar.

Wittgaw. The deed specifies that our author came from Basel and that he worked as a cutler.[8] Indeed in Basel a certain Joachim Meyer was born or baptised on 16 August 1537; it is very probable that this is the person we are dealing with.[9] In that case he would have married at about twenty-three years of age, which is about normal for the period. The father's social status as a papermaker is not incompatible with an education in reading and writing. Basel was furthermore an important city where the young Joachim Meyer would have been able to begin studying fencing and pursue training in the cutler's craft - indeed we find another fencing master who was a Basel cutler in the Strassburg archives in 1558.[10] Nonetheless, the hypothesis of a shared name cannot be totally ruled out: indeed there is a Joachim Meyer, a citizen of Sélestat, at the same time as our author.[11] It is probably in the context of his tour as a journeyman that Joachim Meyer came to Strassburg where, like many other journeymen of the period, marriage allowed him to establish himself as a cutler.[12] Indeed he was granted Strassburg citizenship

---

8 *Joachim meÿer v[on] Basel messerschmid* (Microfilm 5Mi482/12 of the Archives of the Parish of St William of Strassburg).

9 Archives of the Parish of St Alban. Joachim Meyer was the son of Jakob Meyer, papermaker, and Anna Freund. On 24 September 1571 his widowed mother was married for a second time, to the papermaker Anton Mey (*Nouveau dictionnaire de biographie alsacienne*, p. 2641).

10 AS 1R21, fol. 446r.

11 AS 1R34, fol. 576r. On 20 August 1569, the widow of Joachim Meyer of Sélestat, who had died in the service of the Duke of Orange, asked for assistance from the Council and the Twenty-One to recover money deposited at Strassburg.

12 On the subject of the journeyman tour and on the artisanal establishment at Strassburg, see Fuchs, 'L'immigration

on 10 June 1560, shortly after his marriage.[13] There appears to have been a child from this union, but the evidence is uncertain.[14]

All the sources agree on his profession as a cutler (*Messerschmidt*), which he practised to the end of his life. This activity was probably the reason for his coming to Strassburg. In addition to the marriage document, it is this profession that is emphasised before the Council and the Twenty-One in 1567 and 1568.[15] This profession is also indicated in the notice of acquisition of the right of citizenship of Hans Küele, also a cutler, who married Meyer's widow, Apollonia Rülmann. Meyer was also selected for a post as accountant or verifier of accounts for the year 1570 in the Company of Smiths.[16]

However, it is not his activity as an artisan but as a fencer that left the most traces in the archives. Multiple times he requested and obtained authorisation to organise fencing contests (*Fechttschuol*), specifically in February 1561, September 1563, June 1566, February 1567, and June 1568. These fencing contests were public spectacles (contrary to what the name might indicate - literally 'fencing schools'). Competitors faced off in pairs to win money. These prizefights were a source of

---

artisanale'.

13 Stehlé, *Le deuxième livre de bourgeoisie*, fol. 170r.

14 AS 1R38, fol. 442r. The marginal note refers to *Joachim Meygers/Wittwe und Kind* ('Joachim Meyer's widow and child'), but there is no mention of this in the body of the minutes, nor does this child appear in any other sources. It could also refer to a child from Apollonia Rülmann's first marriage.

15 The Council and the Twenty-One were essentially Strassburg's city council. For a succinct description of Strassburg institutions, see Mariotte, *Les sources manuscrites*, p. 7.

16 XI138, Register of the Company of Smiths, 1570.

disorder, and the Strassburg authorities required that express permission be sought to organise them. This is particularly clear in the council minutes, for example those of Saturday, 4 September 1563:

> Joachim Meyer, a citizen and cutler, requests authorisation to hold a fencing contest. Decision: granted.[17]

Unfortunately most of these notices include little in the way of additional information. Nonetheless, two notable cases stand out from the rest. In 1561, we learn that a certain Christoph Elias, who also requested permission to organise a fencing contest, was a student of Meyer's (*von Joachim meiern gelert*).[18] Thus by 1561 Joachim Meyer was teaching fencing in Strassburg. Another notable case is the final one, that of 1568. This year our fencer had to repeat his request one week later because he could find no place to meet other than the private residence of a canon of the cathedral chapter.[19] However, a decision of the Council and the Twenty-One on 27 August 1567 forbade holding these fencing contests at the dwellings of canons. In the end, the Council and the Twenty-One reluctantly agreed to make an exception, since notices advertising the contest had already been posted.

---

17 AS 1R26, fol. 352v, Sat. 4 Sept. 1563. The complete transcription is at the end of this article.

18 AS 1R24, fol. 57r, Sat. 15 Feb. 1561.

19 The exact term is *Thumherr hoff*. The minutes specify the person who owned the residence, a certain Cuno von Manderscheid, a relative of the bishop. It should be noted that, although Strassburg Cathedral was reserved for Protestant worship from 1529, the bishop of Strassburg and cathedral canons remained Catholic.

It is difficult to know when Joachim Meyer began composing his fencing treatise, which he dedicates to Johann Casimir, Count Palatine of the Rhine and duke in Bavaria. The book was printed by the printer Thiebolt Berger in Strassburg in 1570, and the prologue is dated 24 February that same year. Such an extensive treatise must certainly have been begun many months previously. Meyer procured the means to execute a work of extraordinary quality, enhanced by lavish woodcuts. The designs are attributed to Tobias Stimmer, the famed Swiss artist who was working in both Switzerland and Strassburg during this period, though scholars do not believe that Stimmer himself carved the woodcuts.[20] Four monograms – the equivalent of a signature – have been found on five of the woodcuts from the Meyer's book. None of them resembles the known monograms of Tobias Stimmer, three remain anonymous, and one of them has been recognised as the signature of Hans Christoph Stimmer, Tobias's younger brother.[21] The cost of the printing and the execution of the woodcuts compelled Joachim Meyer to go heavily into debt: he promised to repay 300 crowns before Christmas 1571.[22]

At Speyer in 1570, he established a contract with Duke Johann-Albrecht I of Mecklenburg-Schwerin, engaging himself as a fencing master. Joachim Meyer thought he might sell his books for a higher price at the Duke's court

20 Nagler and Andresen, *Monogrammisten*, vol. 4, p. 519.

21 Nagler, *Künstler-Lexicon*, vol. 11, pp. 363–5.

22 Two gold pieces known as crowns were recognised in the Empire around 1570: the French crown 'of the sun', valued at 93 Kreutzers, and the so-called Italian crown, valued at 91 Kreutzers; there was also a silver one. By comparison, a Thaler or Reichsthaler was worth between 68 and 72 Kreutzers at the same time. See Hanauer, *Études économiques*, pp. 255–9.

in Schwerin, more than 30 florins each. Perhaps he also took advantage of the Imperial Diet that took place at Speyer in June 1570 to approach numerous noblemen. He sought and obtained permission from the Strassburg authorities to leave the city[23] - doubtless in order to avoid losing his citizenship. He sent the books in a chest to Schwerin. Then after receiving funds from the Duke, he left Strassburg on the Thursday after Oath-Day (*Schwörtag*, which always took place the first Tuesday of the year) in January 1571.[24] He arrived at the Duke's court on 10 February, and died 24 February: 'Almighty God reclaimed him, and ordered him to leave this vale of tears and to rejoin Him in eternal life.'[25] The cause of death is not specified in any of the sources I have examined, but one might imagine (as his brother-in-law suggested) that the voyage of about 800 km (500 miles) in the middle of winter was in part responsible.[26]

Epilogue

The Duke informed Meyer's family of his death.[27] Antoni Rülmann, Joachim Meyer's brother-in-law, became

---

23 AS 1R38, fol. 442r. Antoni Rülmann, his brother-in-law, indicates in his petition that a suit in the city had brought about his downfall. I have not found confirmation of this point in the minutes.

24 *Schwörtag* was an annual ceremony where the new officers took the oath and read the constitution in public (Mariotte, *Les sources manuscrites*, p. 70).

25 Extract translated literally from Antoni Rülmann's letter to the Duke of Mecklenburg-Schwerin (AS V14, document 110).

26 The city of Schwerin is located in northern Germany, about 100 km (62 miles) east of Hamburg.

27 This document is not preserved in the Strasbourg archives, but the letter is mentioned by Rülmann in his letter to the Duke.

the guardian (*Vogt*) of his sister, Apollonia, Joachim's widow, and took over his debts. On 14 May 1571, he addressed a petition to the Council and the Twenty-One in which he asked that the city of Strassburg assist him in his approaches to the Duke to recover Joachim Meyer's goods, and above all the books. A long-term secretary of the city[28] composed a letter on 15 May to this effect, inviting the Duke to purchase the books if he wished. On 1 July the Duke responded that he had opened the chest containing the books, but that water had damaged all the copies. He indicated that he had paid the shippers, and undertaken to return Joachim Meyer's clothing for 15 Thalers, and that in addition he was sending 50 Thalers to the fencing master's widow. On 1 August 1571 this letter was read before the council, who confirmed the due reception of these effects by the widow. These two letters, that of Antoni Rülmann and the Duke's response, are preserved in the Strasbourg municipal archives; it is thanks to these that we know about the cost of publication, the engagement by the Duke, and the date of Joachim Meyer's death.

For her part, Apollonia Meyer, née Rülmann, was married for the third time on 14 April 1572, to Hans Küele.[29]

The woodcut blocks used for Joachim Meyer's book were probably sold to discharge his debts. They reappeared in Augsburg, one of the principal centres

28 The handwriting of document 110 is identical to that of certain minutes of the Chamber of the Twenty-One: for example, AS 1R34, fol. 576, dating to 1569.

29 Such remarriages were very common in Strassburg at this period. Between 1561 and 1568 widows represented 41.3 per cent of fiancées (Kintz, *La société strasbourgeoise*, p. 191).

for German fencing in the sixteenth century, where they were reused for the subsequent reprinting.[30]

Princes and Religious Conflicts

In 1570 the city of Strassburg, the Duchy of Mecklenburg-Schwerin, and Johann Casimir, Count Palatine of the Rhine, were resolutely Protestant; Joachim Meyer was probably also of this confession. The Duke's choice of a fencing master of the same sect was doubtless not by chance, in this period of religious tension; however, the study of the influences of the religious wars on fencing in the Renaissance exceeds the scope of this article.

The Duchy of Mecklenburg-Schwerin doubtless had another attraction for Joachim Meyer. In 1487 the Emperor Frederick III had granted the Guild of the Marxbrüder the exclusive right to teach fencing, and anyone who professed to teach fencing found themselves punished if they were not affiliated. It was a Duke of Mecklenburg-Schwerin who first responded and granted the same privilege to another guild, the Federfechter. Günterode, the first author citing Meyer in his treatise of 1579, dedicated his work to the Duke of Mecklenburg-Schwerin,[31] probably the son of Meyer's patron, who had died in 1576. The Duchy and the ducal court at Schwerin certainly offered more opportunities to sell a fencing treatise than many of the other princely courts of the Empire.

---

30 Hils, *Meister Johann Liechtenauers Kunst*, p. 189.

31 All this information is taken from Anglo, *Martial Arts*, p. 92.

Fencing Master or Free Fencer?

The case of Joachim Meyer prompts us to question the use of two titles, free fencer (*Freyfechter*) and fencing master (*Fechtmeister*). Meyer presented himself to the city under both titles: in 1566 as free fencer, and in 1568 as fencing master. In the prologue to his treatise, he describes himself as a free fencer. This is also the title applied to him at the end of the letter addressed to the Duke of Mecklenburg-Schwerin by his brother-in-law. On the other hand, the minutes of the meeting of the Council and the Twenty-One, ruling on the request for aid from his brother-in-law to intervene with the Duke, shows that the Strassburg leaders considered him a fencing master. In his letter of response, the Duke gives him only this title, and not that of free fencer. In the Holy Roman Empire, this title was not granted except under certain rules.[32] Joachim Meyer must not have fulfilled all the conditions, otherwise his brother-in-law would surely have mentioned it in his letter, which is not the case. In this regard, to my knowledge, nothing in the Strasbourg archives allows us to affirm that Joachim Meyer belonged to the fraternity of the masters of arms of St Mark (Sankt Marx Brüderschaft), as one will read in various Internet sites dedicated to this author.

The term of fencing master is ambiguous: it can designate competence, or possession of the right to assume this title, or a professional activity. Probably Joachim Meyer had demonstrated to the Strassburg authorities his experience in arms when he presented himself and was recognised as a fencing master, and it was under this designation that the Duke regarded the employment he had offered. A detailed study

32 Hils, *Meister Johann Liechtenauers Kunst*, pp. 207–39.

would be necessary to fully understand what was meant by the designation of free fencer. Perhaps it was simply a designation for fencers who were not affiliated with a guild, or more precisely with the Guild of the Marxbrüder. Hans-Peter Hils sees here an act of resistance, a rejection of the status of the imperially privileged fencer;[33] Meyer's case does not shed any particular light on this point.

The Environment of Fencing in Strassburg

There does not yet exist a study on this environment. The Council and the Twenty-One held the power to authorise fencing contests in Strassburg, and in council minutes around the year 1570 many citizens of Strassburg organised such events, both before and after Joachim Meyer's departure. Not all of these presented themselves as fencing masters; in this respect Joachim Meyer must doubtless have been part of the local élite, in addition to the fact that we know he was already teaching by 1561. In the period from 1561 to 1570, I have found references to five fencing contests organised by Meyer; only Wygand Brack, another Strassburg fencing master, organised more than him in the same period. A deeper study would perhaps allow us to specify his influence or his role at the local level.

Conclusion

Probably born in 1537, Joachim Meyer died one year after the publication of his fencing book, at the age of only thirty-four years. This premature death probably explains why so little information has been gathered previously on this author, whose work

33 Hils, *Meister Johann Liechtenauers Kunst*, p. 311.

would nonetheless become famous. Numerous areas of obscurity still remain in his life: we know nothing about his apprenticeship in fencing, or so little that we must resort to what he tells us in the first paragraphs of his chapter on the rapier, i.e. that he had learned the use of this weapon from foreigners. But did he travel out of the Empire, or had he taken advantage of the presence of foreign masters in Basel or Strassburg? Nor have I found a trace of his apprenticeship as a cutler in the Strassburg archives; he was already a cutler at the time of his marriage. Perhaps some supplementary information could be obtained in the Basel archives. In the same manner, his presence at Schwerin might also have left some traces, and research in the ducal archives might shed some light on the last weeks of his life. In particular the reasons for his death are not specified in either of the two letters, leaving the door open to a multitude of hypotheses.

Archival Sources

Documents from the municipal archives of Strasbourg (Archives de Strasbourg, AS):[34]

Series V, file 14, documents 110 and 141 are respectively the letters sent by Antoni Rülman and the Duke of Mecklenburg-Schwerin.

Baptismal and marriage records of the parish of St William of Strassburg, microfilm 5Mi482/12.

Minutes of the meetings of the Council and the Twenty-One, 1R22 to 1R35, 1R37 to 1R39. In particular:

34 I would like to thank Mr François Schwicker, archivist, who was of great assistance in deciphering these documents.

1R21, fol. 446r: a master of arms and cutler from Basel asks to organise a fencing contest in 1558;
1R24, fol. 57r: the fencing contest of 1561;
1R26, fol. 352v: the fencing contest of 1563;
1R29, fol. 210r: the fencing contest of 1566;
1R30, fol. 44r: the fencing contest of 1567;
1R30, fols. 529v and 533r: prohibition against organising fencing contests in the individual residences of canons of the cathedral chapter;
1R32, fols. 253r, 261r, and 261v: the fencing contest of 1568;
1R34, fol. 576r: mention of the Joachim Meyer from Sélestat;
1R38, fol. 442r: petition addressed to the Council by A. Rülmann;
1R39, fols. 690r to 691v: reading before the Council of the Duke's response.

The sources explicitly mentioning Joachim Meyer are presented more fully below.

Extracts from Strassburg Records

Below is the list of documents in the municipal archives of Strasbourg that explicitly mention Joachim Meyer, with transcriptions and translations of most of the documents.

Archives of the Parish of St William of Strassburg, microfilm 5Mi482/12

Joachim meÿer v[on] Basel messerschmid /
Apolonia Rülmannin Jakob Wickgaws nachgelassen witwe /
Celebrar[u]nt nuptiae / 4. Junÿ .An. 1560

Joachim Meyer of Basel, cutler, and Appolonia Rülmann, widow of Jacob Wickgaw, celebration of nuptials, 4 June 1560.

2nd Book of Citizenry of Strassburg
Folio 170r, 1560
Joachim Meÿger von Basell hatt d[as] burgrecht empfangen vonn Appolonia Rulmennin weÿlandt Jacob wittich des Becken selig[en] wittwen sein[er] hausfrauwen vnnd will dienen zun schmiden. Actum 10 Junÿ anno [etcetera]60

Joachim Meyer of Basel has received citizenship through Appolonia Rülmann, widow of the late Jacob Wittich, baker, and will serve with the smiths. Enacted 10 June 1560.

Folio 365r, 1572
Hans Küele der Messerschmidt hatt das Burgkrecht Empfang[en] von Appolonia Ruollmännin in weÿlands Joachim Meÿers auch Messerschmidt sellig[en] wittwen seiner ehefrawen vnd dient zu den Schmiden. Act[um] den 14t[en] apprillj A[nn]o [etcetera]72

Hans Küele the cutler has received citizenship through Appolonia Ruollmann the widow of Joachim Meyer, also a cutler, his wife, and serves with the smiths. Enacted 14 April 1572.

Communal Administration, Series V
V14 document 110, 15 May 1571
Antoni Rulman, guardian of Appolonia Meyer, widow of Joachim Meyer, fencing-master, who died shortly after his arrival at the court of Duke Johann-Albrecht

of Mecklenburg at Schwerin, requests that he send to Strassburg the clothing of the deceased, and in particular the copies of his work on the art of wielding arms, published at great cost.

V14 document 141, 1 July 1571

Response of Duke Johann-Albrecht of Schwerin to the widow of Joachim Meyer, fencing master, deceased shortly after having entered in his service.

Archives of the Guilds

XI138 (unpaginated): Register of the Officers of the Company of Smiths, 1570

Rechner ins gericht: … Joachim Meÿger, messerschmidt

Accountant of the Company: … Joachim Meyer, cutler

Minutes of the Council and the Twenty-One, Series R

1R24, fol. 57r, Saturday 15 February 1561

Joachim Meier burg[er] alhie bittet jme
zuuergonnen ein fechttschůl zuhalt[en] des
gleich[en] bittet Christoff Elias derso von
jme Joachim meiern gelert jme vber
acht tag hernach[er] gleich[er] gestelt ein schůl
zuhalten. Erkannt Jnen
beiden iren geberen zulassen doch sagenn
dz sye fursehung thůn dz ordenlich gefochten und
kein Unlust furgehe.

Joachim Meyer, a citizen here, requests permission to hold a *Fechtschule*; likewise Christoph Elias, who studied under Joachim Meyer, asks permission to hold a *Schule* in like manner within the next eight days. Decision: they should both be permitted, but they say that they should take care that the fighting is orderly and that nothing untoward happens.

1R26, fol. 352v, Saturday 4 September 1563

Joachim meyer bürger und messerschmid pitt Jme
ein fechtschühl zühalten, Züerlaübenn. Erkandt
Jme Zülassenn

Joachim Meyer, citizen and cutler, requests permission to hold a *Fechtschule*. It was decided to permit him to do so.

1R29, fol. 226r, Saturday 15 June 1566

Joachim meyger d[er] freyfechtter bitt meyne h[erre]n wöllen
jme vergonnen vnd zůlassen ds er bis Montag
nechst künfftig eyn fechttschůl halten möge. Erkanndt
mann solls jme zůlass[en] doch ds er nuhr wid[er] p[er]son
j [pfenning] nemme, sagen jme h[err] Schenkber h[er] Kniebß

Joachim Meyer the free fencer asks my lords to permit him to hold a *Fechtschule* between now and next Monday. It is decided that he shall be permitted to do this, but Master Schenkber and Master Kniebs tell him that he must take only one Pfennig for each person.

1R30, fol. 44r, 1 February 1567

Wygand Brack der fechttmaister bitt meyne herren
wöllen jme erlaůben bis Montag vber achtt tag
eyn offene freye fecthtschůl zuhalten. Allso bitt aůch
Joachim meyger der Messerschmidt jme eyn fechtschůl
zů erlauben, so wöll er Samuel Schilling zu so aůch

zůgegen freyen, derselbig bitt jme allß dann aůch eyn
fechtschůl zu zulassen. Erkanntt
mann solls Wygand Bracken bis montag vber achtt
tag, Joachim Meyger bis Montag über vier=zehen
tag eyn fechttschůl zuhalten zulassen, daby sagen ds
sy es dahin rechtten, Das Es gesellisch freündlich vnd
bescheidenlich abgang, mann werd geburlich
auffsehens haben. Den dritten betreffendt soll
manns zů disem mal gestellen, jst jme hernach[er]
was angelegen mag er wider ansuch[en]

Wygand Brack, the fencing master, asks that my lords permit him to hold an open free *Fechtschule* between now and a week from Monday. Joachim Meyer the cutler also asks to be permitted to hold a *Fechtschule,* and he also asks leave to give permission to Samuel Schilling, who has asked permission of him to hold a *Fechtschule.* It is decided that Wygand Brack shall be permitted between now and a week from Monday, and Joachim Meyer two weeks from Monday; they also say that they must ensure that it takes place in a companionable, friendly, and orderly fashion, with due oversight. The third concerned party is to hold off for the time being, but if he has occasion later he may ask again.

1R32, fol. 253r, 23 June 1568
Weygandt Brack der fechttmaister bitt jme zuerlauben biß
Montag vber acht tag eyn freye offne fechttschul zuhalt[en]
Allso bitt auch Joachim Meyger der fechttmaister jme zuzu=
lassen, biß kunfftigen Montags eyn freye offne fechttschul
zuhalten. Erkanndt weyl sy bede burg[er] soll
manns jnen zulassen, doch dß sy von eyner person nitt
mer dann eyn pfennig nemmen vnd sich fridlich

vnnd bescheidenlich halten. So by eyns Rhats [...]
sagen jnen h[err] Jörg Schoner vnnd heynrich Sypell.

Wygand Brack, the fencing master, requests permission to hold a free open *Fechtschule* between now and a week from Monday. Likewise Joachim Meyer the fencing master also asks permission to hold a free open *Fechtschule* between now and next Monday. Since they are both citizens of Strassburg, it is decided that this should be permitted, but they should take no more than a Pfennig per person, and should conduct themselves peacefully and orderly. Thus is said to them by masters Jörg Schoner and Heinrich Sypell.

1R32, fols. 261r to 261v, 28 June 1568
Joachim Meyger der Messerschmidt vnnd Weygandt
Brack die beden fechttmaister supplicieren an meyne
heren, dennach jnen beden zwo vndeschiedliche fechtt=
schuolen zuhalten erlaubt daby aber vndesagt werden
de jme keyns Thumbheren hoff zuhalt[en]. Sy abe[r]
keyne zunfftstuben bekhommen konnen, hab graff
Chuono von Mondersch[eid] jnen bewilligt. Weyl
denn sy der schuol deselbig zuhalt[en] schon auff geschlag[en]
vnndt mann meyne heren diener gern zulassen,
denhalb keyn mangel erscheynen werde. So bitten
sy jnen zuuergonnen, ds sy zu disen mal die schuol
jne den gemelten Thumbherenhoff halten mugen.Erkanndt.
Dweyl sy sonst keynen platz bekhommen
mugen soll manns jnen jezmal zulassen jnn des
Thumbherenhoff zuhalten / doch daweben sagen meyne
heren haben mißfallen ds sy trage frage die fechtschuol
an dem one angestelle, sagen jnen h[err] Sixt Baltner
vnd Sebastian Scheschtt

Joachim Meyer the cutler and Wygand Brack, both being masters of arms, have submitted a petition to my lords, to be allowed each to hold a separate *Fechtschule*; this was granted to them, but they are forbidden to hold it in a canon's residence. However, they were able to get no suitable rooms, except for what Count Cuno von Manderscheid granted them. Since they have already put up notices that they would hold this *Schule* and one may well grant it to my lords' servants, to avoid a failure, they ask permission this once to hold the *Schule* in the aforesaid canon's residence. It decided, since otherwise they can get no place, that this time they will be allowed to hold it in the canon's residence, but my lords say that they are not pleased that a *Fechtschule* was advertised without prior arrangements, masters Sixt Baltner and Sebastian Schescht tell them.

1R38, fol. 442r

Assistance granted to Antoni Rülmann to intercede with the Duke of Mecklenburg and recover the books of his brother-in-law, Joachim Meyer.

1R39, fols. 690r to 691v

Reading of the response of the Duke of Mecklenburg regarding the return of Joachim Meyer's belongings.

Bibliography

Published Versions of Meyer's Works

Kiermayer, Alexander. *Joachim Meyers Kunst des Fechtens. Gründtliche Beschreibung des Fechtens, 1570. Teil 1 Schwert und Dussack*. Salzhemmendorf: Arts of Mars Books, 2012.

Landwehr, Wolfgang. *Joachim Meyer 1600: Transkription des Fechtbuchs Gründtliche Beschreibung der freyen Ritterlichen und Adelichen kunst des Fechtens*. Herne: VS-Books, 2011.

Meyer, Joachim. *Gründtliche Beschreibung der freyen ritterlichen unnd adelichen Kunst des Fechtens in allerley gebreuchlichen Wehren mit vil schönen und nützlichen Figuren gezieret und fürgestellet. Durch Ioachim Meyer, Freyfechter zu Strassburg*. Strassburg: printed by Thiebolt Berger, 1570.

Meyer, Joachim. *Gründtliche Beschreibung der freyen Ritterlichen und Adelichen Kunst des Fechtens in allerley gebreuchlichen Wehren, mit schönen und nützlichen Figuren gezieret und fürgestellet*. Augsburg: printed by Michael Manger for Elias Willer, 1600.

Meyer, Joachim. *The Art of Combat: A German Martial Arts Treatise of 1570*. Rev. ed. Transl. Jeffrey L. Forgeng. London: Greenhill Books; New York: Palgrave Macmillan, 2015.

Meyer's Manuscripts

The Art of Sword Combat (c. 1568). Lunds Universitetsbibliothek, Msc. A 4o 2.

Rostock Fechtbuch (c. 1565–70). Rostock Universitätsbibliothek, Mss. var. 82.

Other Manuscripts

Döbringer Fechtbuch (1389). Nuremberg, Germanisches Nationalmuseum Cod. Ms. 3227a. Hils no. 41.

Günterode, Heinrich von [Henricus à Gunterrodt] (1579). *Sciomachia et Hoplomachia, sive De veris principiis artis dimicatoriæ.* Dresden, Sächsische Landesbibliothek MS Dresd.C.15. Not in Hils.

Lecküchner, Johannes (1482). *Fechtbuch.* Munich, Bayerische Staatsbibliothek Cgm 582. Hils no. 33.

Lew Fechtbuch (c. 1450). Augsburg, Universitätsbibliothek Cod. I.6.4o.3. Hils no. 5.

Mair, Paulus Hector (c. 1550–55). *Fechtbuch.* 2 vols. Vienna, Österreichische Nationalbibliothek Cod. Vindob. 10825/26. Hils no. 51.

Mair, Paulus Hector (c. 1550–55). *Fechtbuch.* Munich, Bayerische Staatsbibliothek Cod. icon. 393.

Ringeck Fechtbuch (?c. 1440). Dresden, Sächsische Landesbibliothek Mscr. Dresd. C 487. Hils no. 16.

Speyer Fechtbuch (1491). Salzburg, Universitätsbibliothek M. I. 29. Hils no. 43.

Starhemberg Fechtbuch (1452). Rome, Biblioteca dell'Academica Nazionale dei Lincei e Corsiniana Cod. 44 A 8 (Cod. 1449). Hils no. 42.

Other Published Works

Amberger, J. Christoph. *The Secret History of the Sword: Adventures in Ancient Martial Arts*. Burbank, CA: Unique Publications, 1998.

Amman, Jost. *Jost Ammans Stände und Handwerker*. Munich and Leipzig: Hirth, 1923.

Anglo, Sydney. *The Martial Arts of Renaissance Europe*. New Haven, CT: Yale University Press, 2000.

Anon. [von Scheiger]. 'Über Dusaken'. *Zeitschrift für historische Waffenkunde* vol. 1, no. 11 (1899), p. 290.

Bauer, Matthias Johannes. 'Die unbekannte illustrierte Fechthandschrift des Hugold Behr. Vorbemerkungen zur Edition von Rostock UB Mss. var. 83 (16. Jhd.).' *Medium Aevum Quotidianum* vol. 55 (2007), pp. 80–5.

Beaujean, Dieter and Paul Tanner. *Abel Stimmer and Tobias Stimmer*. The New Hollstein German Engravings, Etchings and Woodcuts, 1400–1700, vol. 79. Ouderkerk aan den Ijssel: Sound & Vision Interactive, 2014.

Becker, Carl and Rudolph Weigel. *Jobst Amman, Zeichner und Formschneider, Kupferätzer und Stecher*. Leipzig: R. Weigel, 1854.

Bendel, Max, *Tobias Stimmer: Leben und Werke*. Zürich and Berlin: Atlantis-Verlag, 1940.

Blasco, Almudena, Fabrice Cognot, Christine Duvauchelle, Michel Huynh, and Iaroslav Lebedynsky. *L'*épée: *usages, mythes, et symboles*. Paris: Grandpalais, 2011.

Boccia, Lionello G. and Eduardo T. Coelho. *Armi Bianche Italiane*. Milan: Bramante, 1975.

Boeheim, Wendelin. *Handbuch der Waffenkunde*. Graz: Akademische Druck- und Verlagsanstalt, 1966.

Capwell, Tobias, ed. *The Noble Art of the Sword: Fashion and Fencing in Renaissance Europe 1520–1630*. London: Paul Holberton/The Wallace Collection, 2012.

Châtelet-Lange, Liliane. *Strasbourg en 1548: Le Plan de Conrad Morant*. Strasbourg: Presses Universitaires de Strasbourg, 2001.

Demmin, Auguste. *Weapons of War*. London: Bell and Daldy, 1870.

Demmin, Auguste. *Die Kriegswaffen in ihren geschichtlichen Entwickelungen von den ältesten Zeiten bis auf die Gegenwart: eine Encyklopädie der Waffenkunde*. Leipzig: P. Friesehahn, 1893.

Deutsches Klingenmuseum Solingen. *Deutsches Klingenmuseum Solingen: Führer durch die Sammlungen*. Köln: Rheinland-Verlag, 1991.

Dolínek, V. and J. Durdík. *The Encyclopedia of European Historical Weapons*. London: Hamlyn, 1993.

Dufty, Arthur Richard. *European Swords and Daggers in the Tower of London*. London: HMSO, 1974.

Dupuis, Olivier. 'Joachim Meyer, escrimeur libre, bourgeois de Strasbourg (1537?–1571).' In *Maîtres et techniques de combat à la fin du Moyen Âge et au début de la Renaissance*, ed. Fabrice Cognot. Paris: Association pour l'Edition et la Diffusion des Études Historiques, 2006, pp. 107–20.

Egenolff Fechtbuch. *Der Altenn Fechter anfengliche Kunst*. Frankfurt-am-Main: Christian Egenolff, ?c. 1535.

Forgeng, Jeffrey L. 'Joachim Meyer: Encyclopédiste du Combat Médiéval.' *L'Art de la guerre* vol. 1, no. 1 (April–May 2002), pp. 20–7.

Forgeng, Jeffrey L. '"Owning the Art": The German *Fechtbuch* Tradition.' In *The Noble Art of the Sword: Fashion and Fencing in Renaissance Europe 1520–1630*, ed. Tobias Capwell. London: Paul Holberton/The Wallace Collection, 2012, pp. 164–75.

Forgeng, Jeffrey L. *The Art of Swordsmanship by Hans Leckũchner*. Woodbridge: Boydell and Brewer, 2015.

Forgeng, Jeffrey L. and Alexander Kiermayer. '"The Chivalric Art": German martial arts treatises of the Middle Ages and Renaissance.' In *The Cutting Edge: Studies in Ancient and Medieval Combat*, ed. Barry Molloy. Stroud: Tempus Books, 2007, pp. 153–67.

Fuchs, François Joseph. 'L'immigration artisanale à Strasbourg de 1544 à 1565.' In *Artisans et ouvriers d'Alsace*. Publications de la Société Savante d'Alsace et des Régions de l'Est 9. Strasbourg: Istra, 1965, pp. 185–95.

Führer durch das königlich Bayerische Nationalmuseum in München. Munich: Akademische Buchdruckerei von F. Straub, 1882.

Grimm, Jacob and Wilhelm Grimm. *Deutsches Wörterbuch*. Leipzig: S. Hirzel, 1860.

Günterode, Heinrich von [Henricus à Gunterrodt]. *De veris principiis artis dimicatoriæ tractatus brevis, ad illustrissiumum principem Joannem ducem Megapolensem*. Wittenberg: Mattheus Welack, 1579.

Hanauer, Auguste. *Études économiques sur l'Alsace ancienne et modern. Tome Premier: Les monnaies*. Paris: A. Durand; Strasbourg: Simon, 1876.

Hils, Hans-Peter. *Meister Johann Liechtenauers Kunst des langen Schwertes*. Frankfurt am Main and New York: P. Lang, 1985.

Kintz, Jean-Pierre. *La société strasbourgeoise du milieu du XVIe siècle à la fin de la guerre de trente ans, 1560–1650*. Paris: Ophrys, 1984.

Krenn, Peter. *Schwert und Spiess = Swords and Spears.* Graz: Kunstverlag Hofstetter, 1997.

Krenn, Peter and Kurt Kamniker. 'Die Dusäggen des Landeszeughauses in Graz.' *Waffen- und Kostumkunde* vol. 15, no. 2 (1973), pp. 139–45.

Kunstmuseum Basel. *Spätrenaissance am Oberrhein. Tobias Stimmer 1539–1584. Ausstellung im Kunstmuseum Basel 23. September–9. Dezember 1984*. Basel: Kunstmuseum Basel, 1984.

Laking, Sir Guy Francis. *A Record of European Armour and Arms through Seven Centuries*. 5 vols. London: G. Bell and Sons, 1920–22.

Landeszeughaus am Landesmuseum Joanneum. *Schwert und Säbel aus der Steiermark*. Graz: Landeszeughaus, 1975.

LaRocca, Donald J. 'The Renaissance Spirit.' In *Swords and Hilt Weapons*. New York: Weidenfeld and Nicolson, 1989, pp. 44–57.

LaRocca, Donald J. *The Academy of the Sword: Illustrated Fencing Books 1500–1800.* New York: Metropolitan Museum of Art, 1998.

Leng, Rainer. *Katalog der deutschsprachigen illustrierten Handschriften des Mittelalters Band 4/2, Lfg. 1/2: 38. Fecht- und Ringbücher*. Munich: C. H. Beck, 2008.

Liechtenauer, Johannes. 'Der nach Reimzeilen gegliederte Merktext Meister Liechtenauers zum Fechten mit dem Langen Schwert.' In Wierschin, *Liechtenauers Kunst*, pp. 167–73.

Livet, Georges and Francis Rapp. *Histoire de Strasbourg des origines à nos jours.* 4 vols. Strassburg: Istra, 1981.

Lübeck, Wilhelm. *Lehr- und Handbuch der Deutschen Fechtkunst.* Frankfurt an-der-Oder: Gustav Harnecker, 1865.

Marcelli, Francesco Antonio. *Regole della Scherma.* Rome: Antonio Ercole, 1686.

Mariotte, Jean-Yves. *Les sources manuscrites de l'histoire de Strasbourg. Tome I: des origines à 1790.* Strasbourg: Édition des archives municipales, 2000.

Müller, Heinrich and Hartmut Kölling. *Europäische Hieb- und Stichwaffen aus der Sammlung des Museums für Deutsche Geschichte.* Berlin: J. Neumann-Neudamm, 1981.

Murray, John. *Handbook for Travellers in Southern Germany.* London: Clowes and Sons, 1873.

Nagler, Georg Kaspar. *Neues allgemeines Künstler-Lexicon.* Munich: E. A. Fleischmann, 1847.

Nagler, Georg Kaspar and Carl Andresen. *Die Monogrammisten: und diejenigen bekannten und unbekannten Künstler aller Schulen.* Munich: Georg Franz'sch Buch- und Kunsthandlung, 1871.

The New Gallery. *Exhibition of the Royal House of Tudor.* London: New Gallery, 1890.

Norman, A. V. B. *Rapier and Smallsword.* London; New York: Arms and Armour Press; Arno Press, 1980.

North, Anthony. 'From Rapier to Smallsword.' In *Swords and Hilt Weapons.* New York: Weidenfeld and Nicolson, 1989, pp. 58–71.

Nouveau dictionnaire de biographie alsacienne. Vol. 6. Strasbourg: Fédération des Sociétés d'Histoire et d'Archéologie d'Alsace, 1994.

Oakeshott, R. Ewart. *European Weapons and Armour from the Renaissance to the Industrial Revolution.* North Hollywood, CA: Beinfeld Publishing, 1980.

Pacheco de Narváez, Luis. *Nueva ciencia y filosofía de la destreza de las armas, su teórica y práctica.* Madrid: Melchor Sánchez, 1672.

Pallavicini, Giuseppe Morsicato. *La scherma illustrata composta da Giuseppe Morsicato Pallavicini Palermitano*. Palermo: Domenico d'Anselmo, 1670.

Paurenfeindt, Andreas. *Ergrundung ritterlicher Kunst der Fechterey*. Vienna: Hieronmus Vetor, 1516.

Reichsstadtmuseum Rothenburg. *Katalog zur Waffensammlung der Stiftung Baumann in den Räumen des Reichsstadtmuseums in Rotheburg o.d. Tauber*. Rothenburg ob der Tauber: Reichsstadtmuseum Rothenburg, 2010.

Riff, Adolphe. 'La Corporation des Maréchaux de la Ville de Strasbourg de 1563 à 1789.' In *Artisans et ouvriers d'Alsace*. Publications de la Société Savante d'Alsace et des Régions de l'Est 9. Strasbourg: Istra, 1965, pp. 171–84.

Ritter, François. *Histoire de l'imprimerie alsacienne aux XVe et XVIe siècles*. Strasbourg: Le Roux, 1955.

Rösener, Christoff. 'Ehrentitel und Lobspruch.' In *Sechs Fechtschulen (d.i. Schau- und Preisfechten) der Marxbrüder und Federfechter aus den Jahren 1573 bis 1614; Nürnberger Fechtschulreime v. J. 1579 und Rösener's Gedicht: Ehrentitel und Lobspruch der Fechtkunst v. J. 1589*, ed. Karl Wassmannsdorff. Heidelberg: Karl Groos, 1870, pp. 46–58.

Rott, Jean. 'Artisanat et mouvements sociaux à Strasbourg autour de 1525.' In *Artisans et ouvriers d'Alsace*. Publications de la Société Savante d'Alsace et des Régions de l'Est 9. Strasbourg: Istra, 1965, pp. 137–70.

Schneider, H. and K. Stüber. *Waffen im Schweizerischen Landesmuseum: Griffwaffen I*. Zurich: Orell Füssli Verlag, 1980.

Seitz, Heribert. *Blankwaffen*. 2 vols. Braunschweig: Klinkhardt and Biermann, 1965.

Solms-Laubach, Rudolph, Graf zu. *Geschichte des Grafen- und Fürstenhauses Solms*. Frankfurt-am-Main: C. Adelmann, 1865.

Stehlé, Antoine. *Le deuxième livre de bourgeoisie de Strasbourg, 1543–1618*. Strasbourg: Archives municipales de Strasbourg, 2001.

Strobel, A. G. *Histoire du gymnase protestant de Strasbourg*. Strasbourg: Frédéric Charles Heitz, 1838.

Sutor, Jacob. *New Kunstliches Fechtbuch*. Frankfurt-am-Main: Johann Bringern, 1612.

Talhoffer, Hans. *Medieval Combat: A Fifteenth-Century Illustrated Manual of Swordfighting and Close-Quarter Combat*. Transl. and ed. Mark Rector. London: Greenhill Books, 2000.

Thibault, Girard. *Académie de l'espée de Girard Thibault d'Anvers*. Leiden: B. and A. Elzevier, 1628.

Tobler, Christian Henry. *In Saint George's Name: An Anthology of Medieval German Fighting Arts*. Wheaton, IL: Freelance Academy Press, 2010.

Verolinus, Theodorus. *Der Kunstilche* [sic] *Fechter, oder dess Weyland wohl-geübten und berümten Fecht-Meisters Theodori Verolini kurtze jedoch klare Beschriebung und Ausweisung der freyen ritterlichen und Adelichen Kunst des Fechtens im Rappier, Dusacken und Schwerd, wie dann auch mit angehängter Ring-Kunst*. Würzburg: Joann Bencard, 1679.

Walde, Otto Vilhelm Cison. *Storhetstidens Litterära Krigsbyten, en Kulturhistorisk-Bibliografisk Studie*. Uppsala: Almqvist and Wiksells Boktryckeri-a.-b, 1916–20. http://catalog.hathitrust.org/Record/006673945.

Wassmannsdorff, Karl. *Sechs Fechtschulen (d.i. Schau- und Preisfechten) der Marxbrüder und Federfechter aus den Jahren 1573 bis 1614; Nürnberger Fechtschulreime v. J. 1579 und Rösener's Gedicht: Ehrentitel und Lobspruch der Fechtkunst v. J. 1589*. Heidelberg: Karl Groos, 1870.

Wierschin, Martin. *Meister Johann Liechtenauers Kunst des Fechtens*. Munich: Beck, 1965.

Wilczek, Johann Nepomuk, Graf von. *Erinnerungen eines Waffensammlers: Vortrag gehalten am Gesellschaftsabend Österreichischer Kunstfreunde zu Wien den 3. Dezember 1903*. Vienna: Adolf Holzhausen, 1903.